THE ELEMENTS OF THE DRUID TRADITION

Philip Carr-Gomm is Chief of the Order of Bards, Ovates and Druids, having studied with his teacher, the Chief Druid Philip Ross Nichols, from the age of fifteen. He has trained in Psychosynthesis, psychotherapy for adults, and play therapy and Montessori education for children.

The *Elements Of* is a series designed to present high quality introductions to a broad range of essential subjects.

The books are commissioned specifically from experts in their fields. They provide readable and often unique views of the various topics covered, and are therefore of interest both to those who have some knowledge of the subject, as well as those who are approaching it for the first time.

Many of these concise yet comprehensive books have practical suggestions and exercises which allow personal experiences as well as theoretical understanding, and offer a valuable source of information on many important themes.

In the same series

Aborigine Tradition
Alchemy
The Arthurian Tradition
Astrology
Buddhism
The Celtic Tradition
The Chakras
Christian Symbolism
Creation Myth
Dreamwork
Earth Mysteries
Feng Shui
The Goddess
The Grail Tradition
The Greek Tradition

Herbalism
Human Potential
Meditation
Mysticism
Natural Magic
Pendulum Dowsing
Prophecy
Psychosynthesis
Qabalah
Shamanism
Sufism
Tai Chi
Taoism
Visualisation
Zen

THE ELEMENTS OF

THE DRUID
TRADITION

Philip Carr-Gomm

ELEMENT

Shaftesbury, Dorset ● Rockport, Massachusetts
Brisbane, Queensland

© Philip Carr-Gomm 1991

First published in Great Britain in May 1991 by
Element Books Limited
Longmead, Shaftesbury, Dorset

Reprinted August 1991
Reprinted 1992

First published in the USA in 1991 by
Element, Inc.
42 Broadway, Rockport, MA 01966

First published in Australia by
Element Books Ltd for
Jacaranda Wiley Ltd
33 Park Road, Milton, Brisbane, 4064

Cover illustration by Courtney Davis
Cover design by Max Fairbrother
Typeset by Selectmove Ltd, London
Printed and bound in Great Britain by
Biddles Ltd, Guildford and King's Lynn

Note: The Elements of series is printed on part recycled paper

British Library Cataloguing in Publication Data
Carr-Gomm, Philip
The elements of the druid tradition.
1. Druidism
I. Title
299.15

Library of Congress data available

ISBN 1–85230–202–X

*This book is dedicated to Nuinn
and to Sophia, Lawrence and Matthew*

CONTENTS

ACKNOWLEDGEMENTS

To Stephanie, Douglas, Alice, Susan, Simon, Vera, Jay, Julia, Michael, Glynn, Chauncey, Nicholas, Bede, Colin and Liz, John and Caitlín and the many members of the Order whose promptings, gatherings, wisdom and encouragement have led to the writing of this book.

FOREWORD

It is often said – usually by those who have not studied the subject – that the world-view and philosophy of the old Druids is lost beyond recall . . . [but] it is by no means impossible to regain in the present age the spirit of original Druid philosophy. It is essential indeed to do so; for a revival of the old Druidic way of thought, acknowledging the sanctity of the living earth and all its creatures, seems the only alternative to planetary dissolution.

John Michell – *Stonehenge*

I once asked the owner of an esoteric bookstore in New York why he didn't stock any books on the Druids. His reply was immediate and categorical: 'Because nothing is known about the Druids except a few lines from Caesar, and anyone who says that they know anything more is lying!'

Fortunately his statement is incorrect. We know a certain amount about the ancient Druids and a good deal about Druidry, even though the information is scattered, and often obscure or misleading.

The search for a clear understanding of Druids and Druidry is one which is of particular relevance and value at the present time.

Prince Philip, in his speech to a Washington conference on religion and ecology in 1990 said: 'It is now apparent that the ecological pragmatism of the so-called pagan religions . . . was a great deal more realistic in terms of conservation ethics than the more intellectual monotheistic philosophies of the revealed religions.'[1]

As we struggle to find a way of life that ceases the destruction of the environment, and reconnects us to nature as a living Spirit, we are turning again to those pagan religions to which Prince Philip referred.

Apparently buried for centuries and considered as anachronisms, they are now being re-examined and revived with the understanding that our spirituality must, in these ecologically desperate times, be reunited with the earth.

The Druid understanding of life holds the seed and root-wisdom of our forebears. Some, like the New York bookseller, believe this wisdom was lost over a thousand years ago. I have found this to be untrue, and hope to demonstrate this in the coming pages.

I had the tremendous good fortune to meet my Druid teacher when I was very young and just beginning to question the purpose and meaning of life. From the time of that meeting to the present day each particular approach to this questioning that I have experienced has added to my understanding, and far from contradicting the original outlines that he gave me nearly twenty-five years ago, have served only to confirm them.

The first four chapters of this book attempt to answer the questions: Who were and are Druids? The second four chapters: What do they believe and what do they do? In the Introduction I attempt to clarify some of the issues involved in such a study and to point to the possibility that a research into Druidry represents a type of cultural therapy. But before we begin our enquiry let us look at the meaning of the word Druid:

'Among the Celts and Gauls there are people called Druids or Holy Ones.'

Diogenes Laertius

What does the word 'Druid' mean? Where does it come from? In classical texts, it is given only in the plural: as *druidai* in Greek and as *druidae* or *druides* in Latin. In the Old Irish texts druid is the plural for the singular *drui*.

As we shall see, Druidry is a living system that has constantly evolved and changed over time, as it has integrated certain of the influences around it. To tease out the separate influences is difficult and we can never be sure that we have identified these correctly. As this is true for Druidry as a practice or set of beliefs, so this is true for the word Druid itself. Not all scholars are able to agree about its etymology, but most modern authorities agree with the classical authors that the most likely derivation is from the word for oak, combined with the Indo-European root *wid* – to know, giving their translation of the word Druid as 'One with knowledge of the oak' or 'Wise man of the oak'. Support for this derivation is substantial as we can see from the words for oak in the following four languages:

Daur	Irish	Oak (*Drui* – druid)
Dervo	Gaulish	Oak
Derw	Welsh	Oak (*Derwydd* – druid)
Drus	Greek	Oak

Although it may at first sight seem odd that the Druids' knowledge should have been limited to one tree, we can understand that if this is the correct derivation, then the oak will have stood symbolically for all trees, since it was one of the oldest, most prevalent and most revered members of the forest. He who possessed knowledge of the oak possessed knowledge of all the trees. Further support for the idea that the word Druid connects both knowledge and trees is found in the fact that in Irish, trees are *fid* and knowledge *fios*, while in Welsh trees are *gwydd*, and *gwyddon* is a 'knowledgeable one': from which we can suggest that the Druid was one with 'knowledge of the trees' or was indeed a 'wood-sage'.

Further possible sources or influences upon the term Druid are:

Draoi	Gaelic	Magician
Dryad	Greek	Tree or Wood Nymph
Druaight	Manx	Enchantment

Even though we cannot be sure whether these were etymologically involved in the creation of the term, they act as intriguing associations, giving us the image of a Druid as a 'knower of the tree-spirits, knower of magic, knower of enchantment'.

In the postal course on Druidry run by the Order of Bards, Ovates and Druids,[2] the first exercise given is to ask oneself 'What do the Druids and Druidry mean to me?' Part of the appeal of Druidry lies in the fact that the very word itself touches upon archetypes that lie deep within us. Students find that the words are highly evocative, and that if they allow themselves the freedom to make associations, these weave a pattern of words and images that range from magic and mystery to wisdom, heritage, stability and continuity. The practical reason for following the Druid way today lies in the fact that we can contact the potencies hidden behind these words and use them for the benefit of ourselves and others.

But why all this talk only of Druids? Where are the Druidesses? It is a common misperception of Druidry that it is patriarchal. It is true that with the eighteenth-century revival, neo-Druid groups were dominated by male members – as was freemasonry. Although some groups today are still influenced by the patriarchy of the Druid revival period, it is important to understand that this is not authentic Druid practice [if such a thing can be established]. Both Classical and Celtic accounts show that Druidesses as well as Druids existed, and Celtic law gave equality to women – allowing them to choose their own husbands, divorce, own and inherit property, do battle and ascend to chieftainship – as we know well from the story of Boadicea. The modern Order of Bards, Ovates and Druids' membership, for example, is composed equally of both sexes. The word Druid is used throughout this book with the understanding that what is meant is: Druid and Druidess. Although I agree that this decision may continue the myth of gender bias in Druidry, it does make the text easier to read.

There are meditative and imaginative exercises to complement each chapter, for those who would like to try them. These are designed to be carried out in sequence and are given, in a separate section, at the end of each chapter.

Now let us gingerly begin our study of Druids and their lore by seeing how our very approach to them determines whether we discover sages or savages.

INTRODUCTION

The battle over the past is a battle over the future of human culture.
William Irwin Thompson – *The Time Falling Bodies Take to Light*

Trying to understand who the Druids were brings us face to face with a battle between two ideologies – two ways of looking at life: the one materialist, the other spiritual. Our interpretation of history will depend upon which ideology or philosophy we favour, and until we grasp the way in which each stance affects the interpretation of the past, our study of Druids will be confusing in the extreme.

Most books about the Druids have combined factual historical material with esoteric or speculative material in a way that is often unclear and which leads to accusations from academics that the authors have combined fantasy with fact. A smaller number of books have confined themselves to the factual material at their disposal, and have presented their books as objective historical studies of the Druids. But we would be making a great mistake if we thought that the 'objective' books presented the true case, because the underlying ideological stance of the historian intimately affects the way he presents and interprets his data. With Druidry in particular, the data is sparse. It is sufficient for us to form a picture of who they were, and what they did and believed, but it is minimal enough for us to be obliged to rely heavily on interpretation, and in doing this we will be guided by our basic philosophical posture towards life: our understanding of who man really is, and why he is here on this earth.

This is clearly demonstrated when we turn to the most widely read book on this subject, Professor Stuart Piggott's *The Druids*. In this book Professor Piggott is at great pains to be as objective and as 'scientific' as possible as he presents the history of Druidry. He begins by explaining in detail the sources of information we can use for its study, and the constraints and difficulties involved in working with these sources.

He then presents the archaeological and the textual evidence for a study of the ancient past of Druidry, and gives an account of the revival period of Druidry that began in the eighteenth century and continues to the present day. He concludes that in the ancient past, the Druids were 'barbarians' and 'primitives' and he finishes his discussion of their demise in the following way: 'Roman civilization and Celtic barbarism were from the first opposed in structure and temper ... [they were] a casualty in the larger struggle resulting from what Professor Alfoldi called the "Moral Barrier" between two irreconcilable cultures – "the fundamental antithesis between civilized mankind under Roman rule and the world of barbarism on its outskirts" with its "prevalence of vehement instincts and of bestial passions" expressed in such activities as human sacrifice. Druids, bards, seers and the rest had no place in the new Romano-Celtic world which was coming into being in the provinces of the Empire.'

He then opens his study of revival Druidry in this withering way: 'In considering ... the bodies of self-styled Druids which today represent the fag-end of the myth, we enter a world at once misleading and rather pathetic. We may begin our sad pilgrimage through error once again at Stonehenge.'

Reading the conclusions of such an academic, we might well be tempted to abandon our interest in Druidry immediately. Why bother to enquire any further into a body of people who in the past were blood-thirsty barbarians, and who in the present are deluded and pathetic? Unfortunately for Professor Piggott but fortunately for us, it is possible to understand that the conclusions he has drawn from his study of Druidry are dependent almost exclusively on his particular ideology and when presented as 'history' become in themselves dangerously misleading. Piggott's ideology is materialist. He believes that 'Religion is a social artefact, just as are language and literature, houses and pots, domesticated animals or the working of metals. It is brought into being within a society to fulfil certain psychological needs, and is intimately bound up with custom and law, the hierarchies of social structure and the proper functioning of the institutions which define and hold in coherence the society itself.'

This view of religion is known in psychology as a 'bottom-up' theory in which religion is seen as an ideological superstructure

2

created by man out of his needs. The alternative view is the 'top-down' approach – spirituality and the consequent religious structures evolving from it, are seen as emanating from the Divine, from the supernal world, to be received by man as manna, as birthright, as inspiration. Religion arises not from man, but from God, not *from* his needs but in response *to* his needs.

The theological historian would of course understand this distinction, and it is for this reason that theologians such as Matthew Fox and those who attend the annual Conference of Christians and Druids[1] refute Piggott's understanding of Druidry. The student of the esoteric has an even more specific understanding of the top-down approach. It is a well-known occult dictum that the spiritual is causal to the physical – that physical events unfold as a result of spiritual impulses. Those who are unaware of this concept are seen as labouring in the realm of effects – unable to gain a clear picture of history because they do not accept the supra-physical reality of the spirit. Seen in this way, an historical approach which fails to understand the causative nature of the spiritual can be equated with a medical approach which fails to understand the causative nature of spiritual, mental and emotional states on the physical body.

A study of Druidry which fails to make the author's ideological stance clear from the outset will inevitably be misleading. Piggott's book attempts to pass itself off as an objective 'scientific' study, failing to make it clear from the beginning that the author takes a particular view of history which, when understood, is seen to be limited and prejudiced. William Irwin Thompson was right when he said 'History is never a science and rarely an art, and the historian who pretends to the former loses the latter.'[2]

Most other authors approach Druidry with the opposing ideology to Piggott. Whereas Piggott dislikes Druids, ancient and modern, they clearly rather like them. Most favour the top-down approach, without making this explicit. They interpret the historical data in a way that sees ancient Druids as venerable sages, whilst avoiding, almost exclusively, consideration of the Revival Period. Although hard to obtain, being mostly out of print, their books make better reading, but with the exception of Eleanor Merry's *The Flaming Door*, which is so obviously esoteric, they too attempt to pass as objective historical studies.

In writing this book I make no pretence at presenting an objective historical study of the Druids. I hope it will present sufficient historical data to satisfy the enquiring reader, but while trying to be faithful to the 'facts' of the matter, it takes a spiritual, top-down, approach to the subject, espousing an understanding of Druidry shared by most of the classical authors, the antiquarians of the eighteenth-century Druid Revival and those writers who accept the work of Professors Thom, Atkinson, and Hawkins. Just what that understanding is, will hopefully become clear as the book proceeds.

I have discussed Piggott's book in detail, not only because it is the most widely-read book, having gone through several editions and having remained in print for twenty-two years, but also because it provides an excellent example of the major pitfall which lies in wait for those who attempt a study of the Druids. If we could give a voice to the creature who lives at the bottom of this pit, she or he would say this:

> Beware, O mortal, for as you attempt to study the traces left by your forebears, you will be entering a realm of enchantment. You will think that you are studying history, but you will be studying also mythology and science, the depths of human nature and the sources of divine wisdom. At any moment you can be led astray to find yourself wandering through a hall of mirrors that reflect only your own desires and beliefs.

The Druids, and the power that they wielded, lie at the roots of our civilisation. These roots are buried. Most of us are unaware of them – believing that our foundations lie instead in the Judaeo-Christian heritage. When we attempt to explore the foundations of a building or of a psyche we risk severe changes to the superstructure. It is a dangerous business.

For the past twelve hundred years or so we have built layer upon layer over our Druid heritage, until it has been forgotten by the majority of us. As we seek to peel back these layers, we must declare our motives, for if they are unclear or destructive, the guardian of the pit [who is in fact the guardian of the Mysteries, of our psychic and spiritual foundations which will not and must not be violated] will summon us and we will fall into the trap of gazing, not down into the roots, but into a dark mirror which reflects simply our own prejudices. But if our motives are clear, and if we approach the subject with sensitivity, we will find ourselves engaging in what can only be described as cultural therapy. To ease the psychological pain of an individual we need to go back into his past to redeem those moments and those yearnings of childhood which have been forgotten, repressed or denied. To ease the pain and distortions of a culture we also need to examine its past to determine and redeem those dynamics and events which have been repressed, denied and forgotten. Far from being destructive, the work becomes vital and healing.

Never before has this work been so essential. We can no longer fool ourselves that our culture is mature and successful – the evidence is now undeniable that there exist fundamental flaws in its functioning which have resulted in a crisis that threatens the very continuation of many life-forms, including our own. Thomas Berry in *The Dream of the Earth* expresses the crisis in this way: 'It is estimated by highly regarded biologists that between now and the year 2000, in [less than] ten years, in our present manner of acting, we will extinguish possibly between one-half and one million species out of the five to ten million species that we believe presently exist. . . . The change that is taking place on the earth and in our minds is one of the greatest changes ever to take place in human affairs, perhaps *the* greatest, since what we are talking about is not simply another historical change or cultural modification, but a change of geological and biological as well as psychological order of magnitude. We are changing the earth on a scale comparable only to the changes in the structure of the earth and of life that took place during some hundreds of millions of years of earth development.'

Faced with this stark statement of the orgy of destruction we have unleashed on the planet, it becomes imperative to enquire into the roots of our culture, in a last, though perhaps belated, attempt to redeem our forgotten heritage and to transmute the destruction this forgetting has caused into creation – turning humanity's determination to destroy the world into a determination to save it.

1 · WHO WERE THE DRUIDS?

THE ANCIENT PAST

'The first and oldest of things illuminate the last; and immaterial principles are present in material things.'

Iamblichus

Where did the Druids come from? Some say from the West, and some say from the East. Esoteric tradition states that they originated from Atlantis in the West, exoteric scholarship suggests that the Druids as they are known to us in the classical texts evolved as a result of the merging of local neolithic culture with the incoming Celts, who originated in the East.

The esoteric story of Druidry's roots is hauntingly beautiful. The magicians of Atlantis had discovered the secrets of nature and worked in tune with her powers. But some used these same powers for their own ends, to dominate and manipulate others. Eleanor Merry in *The Flaming Door* talks of the struggle between these two groups: 'The War in Atlantis was the war of white against black magic – between those who saw in Nature the great Divine Mother of men and used her gifts for human welfare, and those who saw in Nature the satanic Temptress, offering dark dominion and cruel power.' As catastrophe struck Atlantis, the dark lords were engulfed as they tried to hold on to their temporal powers. The white sages, having greater gifts of foreknowledge and a deeper conviction in the supremacy of spiritual wealth over the material, journeyed both east and west. In the west they landed on the shores of America, in the east, on the shores of Ireland and the western coasts of Britain.

Rudolf Steiner, amongst others, used his clairvoyant powers to observe the events surrounding the fall of Atlantis and the migration of its sages east and westwards. *The Flaming Door* relates Steiner's discoveries to the Druid mysteries, and what Merry terms 'the mission of the Celtic folk-soul'. Christine Hartley, drawing on the teachings of Dion Fortune's Society of the Inner Light, suggests in *The Western Mystery Tradition* that 'we, with our perhaps great[er] inner knowledge, are content to take it that their [the Druids'] wisdom came with the basis of our mysteries from the great Temples of Atlantis.' If we accept this theory of the origin of the early Druids, we are able to understand more readily the reason behind the number of startling similarities that exist between Native American and Druid teachings and practice.

There is no evidence that points to the origin of Druidry stemming from Atlantis in the early literature. However, floods do figure in the Celtic tradition, and in the *Black Book of Carmarthen*, for example, a maiden called Mererid uncovers 'the fountain of Venus' having been raped by Seithennin. The water from the fountain then covers the land.

In Brittany, the story is told of the submerging of Ys. The king's evil daughter worked bad magic, and taking from her father's neck the key of the dyke which protected Ys from the sea, succeeded in drowning both the kingdom and herself in the process.

Both these tales, and certain of the early Grail stories speak of the same events that occurred in Atlantis – a violation of nature resulting in the welling up of waters which inundate the land. The rape of the maiden Mererid, for example, can be seen as a mythic image for the rape of nature engaged upon by the black magicians of Atlantis. The fact that the rape releases uncontrollable waters is symbolically fitting, for it is male analytical consciousness untamed by union with the feminine which exploits the land, and it is the avenging power of the feminine, symbolised by the waters, which is obliged to submerge the unheeding masculine. And it is strange to note how history is apparently about to repeat itself in our age, with the waters of the melted ice-caps rising in response to our rape of the biosphere.

In the *Lebor Gabala Erenn* (The Book of the Taking of Ireland) the biblical flood is documented, but Caitlin Matthews has suggested that in this story and others 'it is perhaps to some vague memory of Atlantis and the spring-guarding maiden that some of the stories look in their primeval vision.'[1] Certainly Celtic tradition speaks of six races who have arrived in Ireland from 'beyond the ninth wave' (the defined boundary of the land beyond which lay the neutral seas): the company of Cessair, the company of Partholon, the people of Nemed, the Fir Bolg, the Tuatha de Danaan and the Milesians. *The Book of the Taking of Ireland* chronicles the invasions of these six races, attempting to integrate bardic memory with biblical tradition, making Cessair the grand-daughter of Noah. But it is the Tuatha de Danaan, the Children of Danu or Dana, the godlike race who have taken refuge in the hollow hills of the *sidhe* with the coming of the Milesians, who are taken by some esotericists to have been the Atlanteans themselves.

Those who favour the Atlantean origins of Druidry suggest that while some of the migrants from the 'Shining Lands' settled in Ireland and Britain, others continued to Asia and India, some by a Northern route, others by a Southern route. Later, the descendants of these migrants flowed back from East to West, and it is this later migration, they suggest, which has been chosen by certain 'exoteric' historians as the focus for their attentions on the origins of Druidry.

Leaving aside the Atlantean theory of origins, whose acceptance is a matter of individual judgement, we can now turn to the more conventional theories of the origins of the Druids, which are based on exoteric historical rather than esoteric or clairvoyant sources of information. We know about the existence of the Druids from the work of the classical authors. The Druids were first mentioned in two separate works dating from about 200 BC and 400 BC respectively that have unfortunately been lost. In the third century AD Diogenes Laertius in the preface to his *Lives of the Philosophers* mentions that the Druids were discussed in a book by the Greek, Sotion of Alexandria, and in a treatise on Magic, ascribed to Aristotle. Historians are confident of the existence of Sotion's book, written in the second century BC, but believe the fourth century BC work of Aristotle to be apocryphal. Taking a mythic or poetic view of the origins of Druidry, it is somehow fitting that we cannot be sure whether the earliest record of this tradition really existed, and that the second earliest record exists not in a library, but in the intangible world where only its memory is recorded over five hundred years after it was written. In this way our knowledge of Druidry rises slowly out of the realm of the Unknown, rather than bursting in on us in a flood of awareness.

EARLY RECORDS

The first record that we have of the Druids that has not been lost is given to us by Julius Caesar in the sixth book of his *Gallic War*, written about 52 BC. We then find a number of classical authors, including, amongst others, Cicero, Strabo, Diodorus Siculus, Lucan, Pliny and Tacitus discussing the Druids, up until about the year AD 385 when Ausonius wrote a collection of odes to the professors of Bordeaux, which includes the story of an old man called Phoebicius, from the Breton stock of Druids, who managed to obtain a chair at Bordeaux through his son's intervention. The work of the classical authors throws a certain, though not comprehensive, light on what the Druids did and believed, and this is discussed in Chapter Four. Transcripts of nearly all their commentaries on the Druids can be found in T. D. Kendrick's excellent book *The Druids*.

The other sources of written information that we have about the Druids come from Ireland, Wales and Scotland. But these are much later in date than the classical sources, and therefore present particular problems of their own when it comes to interpretation. The Irish texts date from the eighth century AD onwards, the Welsh texts were in the main only transcribed in medieval times, and the Scottish material remained in the oral tradition until the late nineteenth century, when folklorists began to document its treasures.

Although not committed to writing until the eighth century, the Irish texts are considered 'an extraordinary archaic fragment of European literature'[2] reflecting 'an older world than any other vernacular literature in western Europe'.[3] They mainly comprise hero-tales and summaries of law codes, and even though transcribed by Christian clerics, they are found to reliably convey a picture of the pre-Christian Druid world of Ireland that existed up until the introduction of Christianity in the fifth century AD.

The Welsh texts, like the Irish, are the written versions of material that was originally transmitted orally. Transcribed much later than the Irish works, the Welsh corpus includes the *White Book of Rhydderch*, which was compiled in about AD 1300 and the *Red Book of Hergest* in about 1400. It is from the *Red Book* that the well-known tales of the *Mabinogion*[4] have been extracted, and a part of this series of tales is also found in the *White Book* – the evidence showing that they were originally committed to writing between AD 1100 and 1250. Another significant Welsh manuscript, which conveys much of the Druid wisdom to us today, is the *Book of Taliesin*.[5]

This is of an even later date, being a seventeenth-century copy of a sixteenth-century manuscript. A further source of knowledge about the Druids and their work comes to us from the *Welsh Triads*,[6] which have been gathered from many manuscript sources. From these we are given an insight into the complex syllabus of bardic training, and through their terse form we can glimpse the depth of bardic and Druidic thought.

The Scottish material, it might be thought, would hardly be reliable as a source of information on the Druids, since it has only been transcribed in this and the previous century. But this material, which includes the massive collection made by Alexander Carmichael, published in six volumes between 1900 and 1961 and entitled *Carmina Gadelica*, serves only to substantiate the understanding of our pre-Christian heritage obtained from the earlier classical, Irish and Welsh sources. It also bears living witness to the extraordinary ability of cultural and spiritual traditions to survive for thousands of years being passed only from mouth to ear. It is true that all these sources of information at our disposal have been affected over time, by Christianity and by continental influences, when the Welsh and Cornish Bards fled to Brittany with the Saxon invasions, returning with changed songs and stories. Despite these influences, the original pre-Christian shape and substance of this material is clearly discernible, and it can be stated that the corpus of material which we have at our disposal for an understanding of Druidry is vast indeed. To this day its riches have yet to be fully researched and appreciated. Even now only about a quarter of the Celtic texts have been translated into English.

ARCHAEOLOGICAL RECORDS

Our knowledge of Druidry can be supplemented, to a small extent, by a study of inscriptions, carving and sculpture. The epigraphic evidence available to us consists of some 360 Ogham inscriptions [see chapter 8], found chiefly on memorial stones in the south-west of Ireland and Wales, dating from the fifth and sixth century AD, and some 374 dedicatory inscriptions, mainly found in Gaul, to Celtic gods or goddesses, although these date almost exclusively from the time when Britain and Gaul formed part of the Roman Empire. The iconographic evidence consists of sculptures and carvings, in both wood and stone, of human and animal forms dating from the sixth century BC. These two sources of evidence, the epigraphic and the iconographic, become illuminating when set within the context provided for us by the textual evidence supported by the findings of archaeology, language studies and comparative mythology. In coming to these sources of evidence we are presented with a rich and exciting field of study which in the last twenty years or so has enabled us to form a picture of Druidry which suggests a continuity of tradition from the neolithic right through to the Celtic era.

Neolithic farming communities dated to 4500 BC have been traced in Southern Britain and Ireland, and as far north as the Orkneys to 3500 BC. It was these 'stone-age' communities who were the megalith builders and who erected their numerous stone monuments during the course of about two and a half thousand years, from 3500 to 1000 BC.

Those of us who have envisaged our neolithic ancestors as 'rude savages' have been forced to radically alter our understanding of them in the light of discoveries pioneered initially by Sir Norman Lockyer at the beginning of this century, but only fully developed in the last twenty years with the detailed surveying and computing work of Professors Thom, Hawkins and Atkinson. This work has shown that the stone circles and other monuments of the neolithic people were erected with an astonishingly sophisticated use of mathematics, which reveals our enlightened ancestors to have been in possession of an understanding of 'Pythagorean' mathematics over a thousand years before Pythagoras was born.

Megalithic remains in the form of burial mounds, standing stones and stone circles have been found all over the world – in Tibet, China, Korea and Japan, in the Pacific Islands, Malaya and Borneo, in Madagascar, India, Pakistan and Ethiopia, in the Middle and Near East, in Africa and the Americas. Due to their similarities of construction, it has been tempting to suggest that these megalith builders originated in one or another place, and that the spread of these sites is due to their migrations. In reality, it is unnecessary to invoke migration theories to explain their ubiquity. The most convincing explanation for their world-wide distribution is found by looking at the arguments of both archeologists and analytical psychologists. Current archaeology suggests that these monuments are similar all over the world because they represent the very simplest of designs – single upright stones, or several uprights supporting a horizontal, as in dolmens and burial chambers. The analytical psychology pioneered by C. G. Jung shows that our own individual consciousness is connected to a collective unconsciousness which results in similar manifestations of the collective human psyche occurring in widely separated parts of the world – no physical connections are required for similar artistic, cultural, religious or architectural phenomena to appear in different regions.

What is known for sure, however, is that the megalithic monuments of western Europe are among the oldest in the world. Carbon-14 dating places the majority of them between the 5th and 2nd millenium BC. Since they are older than the monuments of Africa or Asia, the Near or Middle East they cannot have been 'seeded' from the south or east. Jean-Pierre Mohen says: 'The discovery of this early time scale (in Europe) poses in new terms the question of the genesis of these monuments: we must envisage a local origin for each of the main groups – Iberian, Breton, Irish and Scandinavian.[7]

The neolithic megalith builders of Britain have been termed proto-Druids, in order to distinguish them from the 'historical Druids' known to us from classical texts. I find the word 'proto-Druid' unattractive and prefer the term 'early Druid', even though the prefix 'proto' is accurate enough, meaning 'first-formed' or 'ancestral'. This ancestral Druidry took a major step forward in its development when it merged or inter-acted with the traditions and beliefs of incoming peoples who have been termed 'proto-Celts'.

WHO WERE THE CELTS?

The origins of the Celts is as difficult to determine and as prone to academic disagreement as are the origins of the Druids. Even using the term 'Celt' is fraught with difficulties. Colin Renfrew, Professor of Archaeology at Cambridge, has identified at least eight senses in which the term is used. Renfrew concludes with 'the strong suspicion that the term "Celts" is not a proper ethnic term . . . but was imposed on a wide variety of barbarian tribes by classical geographers.'[8] It is important to understand that he does not deny 'that there was indeed a language group, which since the eighteenth century has been termed "Celtic", nor that there are significant archaeological observations to be made about the material culture and way of life at the relevant places and times.' But he stresses that 'these different and valid perceptions should not be confused by lumping them all together as "Celtic"'[9]

Aware of these cautions, and having insufficient space to review the various theories of Celtic origins, we will simply state that the forebears of the Celts were probably the Beaker folk, who originated either in Central Europe or Iberia in the third millenium BC, and the Battle-Axe folk who almost certainly originated in the steppe-lands of Southern Russia at about the same time. The fusion of these folk in Central Europe in about the second millenium BC resulted in successive cultures known as Unetice, Tumulus and Urnfield. Some scholars argue that towards the close of the second millenium BC the Urnfield culture becomes identifiable as 'proto-Celtic'. From about 700 BC the culture of some of the descendants of the Urnfield people has been labelled Hallstatt, which can safely be regarded as fully Celtic, as opposed to proto-Celtic. The Hallstatt culture is traced for only 200 years, before it gives way to the La Tène culture which survived until the coming of the Romans. If just the Hallstatt and La Tène type of cultures are regarded as Celtic then the Celts only make their appearance in Britain from about 500 BC.

But if we see the ancestors of the Celts as the Beaker and Battle-Axe folk, and term them proto-Celtic as some scholars do, then we can trace the coming of proto-Celts to Britain at least as early as 2000 BC, since Beaker sites in Britain have been identified from about this time.

Professor Renfrew argues against this theory, claiming that although it is favoured by continental archaeologists, 'most [British] archaeologists do not now think in terms of beaker-bearing immigrants on any scale.'[10] Instead Renfrew in a recent work, drawing on studies of historical linguistics, favours a theory of Indo-European origins, which was originally popular in the nineteenth century, but which now, with revised underpinnings, – he re-presents. His arguments are complex and subtle and need to be studied in the original. But they are persuasive. He does not advocate a migrationist model, although he does suggest that before about 6000 BC in the eastern part of Anatolia people speaking languages ancestral to all the Indo-European languages were to be found, and that by 4000 BC the earliest Indo-European speakers would have reached Europe and possibly Britain.

The Celts are seen as originating from these Indo-Europeans. From the sixth millenium BC onwards they expanded from their homelands both east and westward, reaching Britain and Ireland in the west, and India in the east. Studies in comparative mythology show us that Sanskrit literature documents ancient Indian rituals which are similar to those traceable in Celtic Ireland, and there are certain striking parallels which can be drawn between some Hindu deities and Celtic gods.[11] Further similarities can be traced amongst the religious traditions of the Indo-Europeans which help to give us a picture of Druidic practice that can be said to reach back in its origins to the very beginnings of Indo-European culture before 6000 BC. These similarities relate to the sanctity and importance of water; the probable offering of sacrifices; the religious symbolism

Figure 1 The house of a Druid. The roundhouse with its central fire and conic structure was used in Iron-Age and Celtic settlements.

of weapons; the use in some areas of circular and spiral motifs in religious art; a concern for calendrical and probably astrological observation; the sanctity of fire; and the sacred nature of the number three.

Historians used to claim that the Celts came to Britain in a series of invasions from about 500 BC, and that the Druids, being Celts, could not therefore have built the stone circles. The antiquarians of the eighteenth-century Druid Revival and the modern Druid Orders who claimed that the Druids worshipped at such places as Stonehenge were scorned by academics who believed that the completion of the stone circles antedated the arrival of the Celts by over five hundred years. The evidence available to us now, however, shows the Revival and modern Druids to be right about their ancient forebears, whether we consider the proto-Celts to have emerged in Britain in around 2000 BC, as Beaker Folk, or even earlier as Indo-Europeans, as Colin Renfrew argues.

A balanced view of the evidence suggests that Druidry is best conceived as a Tradition, a set of beliefs and practices, whose roots lie both in the Indo-European ancestors of the Celts, and in the native megalithic culture. Both undoubtedly carried with them a formidable corpus of mathematical, astronomical, engineering and philosophical knowledge which fused together in Ireland and Britain and probably only subsequently in Gaul, to form the powerful and multi-faceted

14

group of Bards, Ovates and Druids that are referred to in the classical texts.

Further historical analysis of Druidry's origins is outside the scope of this book. Controversies have raged over virtually every aspect of its early history. For the sake of brevity I have adopted a 'broad-brush' approach, hoping that readers who find the subject intriguing will be able to negotiate their way through the references given in the chapter notes and the books given in the bibliography, to arrive at their own understanding of Druidry's origins and early history, and to come to their own appreciation of the treasures to be found in a study of both the Celtic and megalithic periods.

We are approaching an exciting time in an understanding of our cultural roots: we are simultaneously discovering both the foundations that lie beneath our Judaeo-Christian heritage, and the foundations that lie beneath our Celtic heritage. As if in response to the urgency of our times, two veils are being lifted – the one repressed by our Christian world-view that taught that all that was pre-Christian was 'heathen' and unworthy of our attention; the other repressed by the prejudices of our historians who, influenced by Darwinian concepts of the Rise of Man, espoused the *Urdummheit* [original stupidity] theory of human origins, which refuses to conceive of our ancestors as being possessed of a philosophical, spiritual or even mathematical culture that was in any way sublime.

EXERCISE – 1

Having read this chapter, spend a few moments forgetting all that you have read, making yourself comfortable, and allowing yourself to come to a sense of inner centredness and calm. For meditation we can be seated cross-legged on the floor or in the usual upright sitting position on a chair. Some Western esoteric teachings state that to sit cross-legged on the ground is an Eastern posture inappropriate for Western meditation. This is incorrect. The cross-legged position is depicted in Celtic art and is therefore not exclusively 'eastern'. It provides a sense of humility, of being in touch with the earth, and of being well grounded. Many people, however, find it difficult to meditate in this position, and prefer to be seated in a chair.

Close your eyes and feel all concerns fall away from you. Often, in Druid ceremonies, having entered the circle, we begin by saying 'We leave outside all disturbing thoughts'. Focus for a little while on your breathing, and then become aware of the sun rising. You might do this by imagining you are on a hillside or mountain top gazing at the horizon. Or you might feel a sun rising in your heart, or your solar plexus or in an internal way that cannot be described in words.

Having bathed in the light and warmth of the sun for a while, become aware of being fully yourself again. Feel full of vitality and strength. Become conscious of your physical body and surroundings, and when you feel ready, open your eyes. Do not stand up quickly – stretch a little before standing up or continuing with the next chapter.

2 · THE RECENT PAST
DRUIDRY REBORN

The English poets have some odd things to say of the Druids. Drayton's are drawn through the air by dragons; Milton calls on Parliament to follow the example of the Druids; Pope's Druids may be taken for Scythian heroes; Marvell and Wordsworth picture themselves as Druids, Collins calls Thomson a Druid, and Blake calls Adam a Druid.

A. L. Owen – *The Famous Druids*

With the spread of the Roman Empire through most of Europe, Druidry went underground, suffering persecution and massacre. But in Ireland, unconquered by Rome, it was able to survive until the coming of Christianity in the fifth century. From this time until the eighteenth century we hear virtually nothing of Druidry being practised. But the tradition did not die, and its wisdom was not completely lost.

One of the main reasons for this lay in the fact that the Bards were accepted within the new Christian dispensation, and were thereby able to pass on the golden thread up to our own age. Of this fact there is no dispute, even from the most sceptical of historians, such as Stuart Piggott, who is forced by his loyalty to objective data to admit that the eighteenth century Welsh bards: 'even if somewhat fallen on evil days by 1792, were not nonsense. In the Middle Ages, as with their counterparts in Ireland, they had formed part of the traditional Celtic hierarchy with genuine roots in the ancient past of the Celts and Druids.'[1] The Bardic schools continued to function in Ireland up until the seventeenth century, and in Scotland to the beginning of the eighteenth century.

That such a continuity of tradition should exist is impressive, and there are still other ways that show us how Druidry survived the long journey of over a thousand years from the fifth to the eighteenth century. Handed down within the Order are a series of historical 'glimpses' which are intriguing, even though unsupported by documentary evidence: it is said that before the foundation of Oxford University, there flourished a Druid group particularly concerned with alchemy. It was persecuted and perished at some time before 1066. Two hundred years later we learn of a certain Haymo of Faversham, a brilliant Welshman and monk who, whilst working as Franciscan Minister for England in 1238 revived the Druidic forms. On his death, Philip Brydodd in the early thirteenth century founded and named a grove at Oxford in 1245, calling it the Mount Haemus Grove. Druids apparently gathered from many parts of the country and agreed on a common programme.[2]

THE SURVIVAL OF DRUIDRY

Although this information cannot be relied on historically, it rings true because it speaks of key individuals who created rallying points for dispersed practitioners at certain times. Druidry has worked in this way since 1717, with each of the Chiefs of the Order having gathered together a number of people who otherwise would have practised on their own and in historical 'silence'. It therefore seems quite reasonable to assume that during its underground period, isolated individuals and families practised Druidry, and that occasionally a particular figure emerged who rallied some of them around him, breaking for a moment that silence. The role that Oxford plays is intriguing, and Druidry's connections with the Orphic tradition and the Balkans are evoked in the naming of the Oxford Grove, for Mount Haemus was the classical name for the Balkan range which lies in modern Bulgaria. We should remember that the Celts were to be found in the Balkans, together with impressive megalithic sites.

Apart from these items of traditional Order history, we can deduce the fact that Druidry also survived in some form through the practices of those people who became disillusioned with a church increasingly aligned with the state. As politicisation and materialism strangled the spirituality of the church, the native spirituality would have become increasingly important to those members of the population who were close to the earth and far away from the seats of power. Jules Michelet outlined this phenomenon in France, describing how the peasantry turned away from Christianity with the coming of feudalism and the suppression of the popular Celtic church.[3] As the church united the aristocracy and the clergy in tyranny, the people turned to the Old Religion, in an attempt to meet their need for a true spirituality. Whether that Old Religion was Wicca or Druidry or a combination we cannot tell, but what we do know is that pagan customs and practices did survive.

They survived in folk tradition as well as in the more conscious form of actual grove or coven meetings held in secret to avoid persecution. Folk tradition gives us the symbolic dances of the Morris Men, the Helston Furry Dancers and the Abbots Bromley Horn Dancers amongst others. And it gives us a host of ancient customs surrounding each of the festival times.[4]

Just as there are instances of families who claim to have carried the Wiccan traditions in secret from one generation to another, so there are individuals today who claim that their families have preserved the Druid traditions. Priesthood of the Culdee Church was often passed from one generation to the next through inheritance, and there are still families who claim Culdee descent. The Culdee church, as the very first organised church in Britain, was in direct contact with ancient Druidry.

Professor Anne Ross has discovered an entire community in North England which venerates the 'old gods' while still professing and practising Christianity.[5] Its members claim they are of Celtic stock, a remnant who refused to flee during the various migrations. They have succeeded in preserving the ancient earth-wisdom of their ancestors, and it is fitting that the exact location of this community should remain a closely guarded secret, although members have given anonymous interviews on radio and television since Anne Ross's disclosures.

The story of St. Kilda, Britain's remotest island, also shows how Druidry was far from extinguished with the advent of Christianity. Being so isolated in the North Atlantic, the first missionary arrived there in 1705. He found that eight years previously an islander from Skye, Martin Martin, had spent three weeks there and had endeavoured to rid the St. Kildans of some of their ancient religious practices.[6] He apparently persuaded them to destroy several of their altars and stone circles. But Buchan, the missionary, observed that although some of the idolatrous monuments of a physical nature had been destroyed, 'the spiritual ones which were erected in the hearts of the islanders were not touched.' We have a certain amount of information about their beliefs, and we know of both a Druid and a Druidess who lived there – Stallir the Druid who lived on one of St. Kilda's satellites Boreray, and a Druidess, known as the Amazon. She loved hunting and is said to have set her hounds after the deer chasing them across to Harris and Lewis, since in those days there was dry land between St. Kilda and the Outer Hebrides, as indeed there were oak trees [discovered recently through pollen analysis on the now treeless island]. The last inhabitants of St. Kilda evacuated the island in 1930. Those surviving, or their descendants, may well have inherited customs and stories worthy of our attention.

With all these examples of inherited lore there is fertile ground for sensitive research which respects family traditions and secrecy, while recognizing that as we move into the next millenium the time has come for much of that hidden knowledge to become known. Wicca and Druidry are children of our pre-Christian pagan past – like brothers and sisters they come from the same stock of Celtic and pre-Celtic tradition. Wicca has managed to survive through centuries of persecution up to the present day, and it is reasonable to assume that the same has occurred with Druidry. Like siblings who carry related, if not identical, genetic material, both traditions will have preserved aspects of their progenitors. Each has managed to carry the sap from their millenia-deep roots to the flowering that both traditions are experiencing today.

Each of us carries a physical, genetic inheritance and a non-physical, spiritual inheritance of the combined experience of our previous lives. In the same way, a spiritual current, such as Druidry, has both physical transmissions of tradition and spiritual ones. If all books on Druidry and all its current practitioners were to be destroyed, it would still survive to appear again in some form at some time and in some place. Such things a materialist historian cannot understand. Psychologists and physicists might find it easier, with their knowledge of the workings of the collective unconscious and of such phenomena as morphic resonance.[7] Things are never what they appear to be and communication can occur in non-physical ways. This understanding helps us to see that the Druid Tradition did not die with the coming of Christianity, but has remained alive and has been transmitted through the centuries because Druidry, Druids and Druid practice are not simply physical. One of the most striking proofs of this lies in the experiences isolated individuals have of receiving instruction from inner-plane Druid teachers, who convey inspiration and practices which accord precisely with outer-plane Druid practice, even though the individuals concerned knew nothing of outer-plane Druidry. Each successive Chief of the Order has contributed material which he has received from inner-plane contacts to the body of lore handed down to him. In this way, the tree of Druidry grows from within, nourished from a supra-physical source. To recap, we see the threads that link the ancient past of Druidry with its recent past as follows:

Firstly, the 'physical' continuity represented by: (1) the preservation of lore through the Bardic traditions of Wales, Scotland and Ireland; (2) the tradition that key individuals gathered groups together, while individuals and families passed the wisdom and practices down through successive generations; (3) the survival of folk customs and dances; (4) the evidence that the 'Old Religion' was practised in Britain and France when the 'New Religion' of Christianity allied itself with the ruling aristocracies and lost its connection with nature with the suppression of the Celtic Church; and (5) the evidence that isolated rural communities practised paganism and handed on age-old traditions up to the present day.

Secondly, the 'non-physical' continuity, the inner stream of Druid Tradition that flows regardless of outer plane interruptions or restrictions to Druid practice, proven by the fact that individuals can and have received or channelled Druid wisdom from within. Our increasing understanding of non-physical phenomena such as extra-sensory perception and near-death experiences makes this mode of transmission increasingly acceptable even to the scientifically-minded.

To return to the level of the manifest, physical representation of Druidry we need to look at the period which has become known as the Revival Period of Druid history. This began with the Renaissance, when the classical texts dealing with the Druids were rediscovered and eventually printed. By the sixteenth century virtually all of the texts were available to scholars.

THE REVIVAL PERIOD

As the British, French and Germans became intrigued by their pre-Christian ancestry, the discovery of the New World brought them face to face with people who, with their strange way of living, might have resembled their own ancestors. Opinions about the nature of the native Americans were divided: some saw them as blood-thirsty and living in 'continuall feare, and danger of violent death ... [a life] solitary, poore, nasty, brutish and short'.[8] Others found that they 'seem to live in that golden worlde of whiche the old writers speake so much ... the golden worlde without toyle'.[9] In 1584 Arthur Barlowe found the Virginian Indians 'most gentle, loving and faithfull, void of all guile, and treason, and such as lived after the manner of the golden age'. A related opposition of views prevailed with regard to Druidry. Some saw the Druids as evil and primitive human sacrificers, while others saw them as peace-making sages and philosophers, presiding over a corpus of teaching as dignified as that of the Greeks or the Brahmins.

This polarisation of views continues to this day. Ask a friend what comes to mind when she or he thinks of Druids, and one will tell you that they think of wise men, guardians of inner wisdom, while another will tell you that they think of virgins being sacrificed by Druids on the 'slaughter stone' of Stonehenge.

These images go back, of course, to the reports of the classical authors themselves, who conveyed both images to our present-day minds. But the relationship between the Druid Revival and the discovery of the New World and its inhabitants is far more significant if we observe it from an esoteric standpoint. Tradition states that the Druid and the Native American traditions arose from the same source – Atlantis. Thousands of years later both Druidry and the native traditions emerge out of obscurity at about the same time. Three hundred years on, the current revival of interest in Druidry coincides with the resurgence of interest in the Native American traditions. Clearly the Druid and Native American ways are related esoterically in ways we can hardly comprehend.

To return to exoteric history, we see that in Germany and France, the availability of the classical texts enabled a vision of their pre-Roman past to emerge that was noble rather than savage. The deep-seated urge to honour one's origins manifested itself in a patriotic pride in these early philosophers: and from 1514 onwards, a series of eulogistic accounts of both Gaulish and German Druids appeared on the Continent. In Britain, although Druids appeared on stage for the first time in Fletcher's *Bonduca* of 1618 and mention was made of Druids in works such as Drayton's *Polyolbion* of 1622 and Milton's *Lycidas* of 1637, it was not until the 1690s that the Druid Revival began in earnest when John Aubrey, the writer and antiquarian, turned his attention to the stone monuments of Wiltshire.

Aubrey, having studied the classical references to Druidry, carried out pioneering field-work at the great monuments of Avebury and

*Figure 2   John Aubrey, writer and antiquarian (1626 – 1697) founder
in spirit, and perhaps in fact of the modern English Druid movement.*

Stonehenge. Many of his contemporaries regarded them as of Roman
or of later date, but Aubrey realised they were far more ancient and
that they were ceremonial centres. He concluded that they were
probably used by the Druids. He began work on a book, originally
entitled *Templa Druidum*, but later changed as its scope widened to
Monumenta Britannica. Although only excerpts were ever published,
the effect of his work was to forge an association between Stonehenge
and the Druids, which lives in the minds of most people to this
day. In the previous chapter we have seen how the latest research
makes this association perfectly legitimate. But as recently as the
mid 1960s many academics deemed it spurious, prompting Stuart
Piggott to write: 'In Aubrey's tentative association of Stonehenge
and other prehistoric stone circles with the Druids was the germ of
an idea which was to run like lunatic wildfire through all popular
and much learned thought, and particularly emotive feeling, until
modern times.'[10]

In many ways John Aubrey can be seen as the real founder of the modern Druid movement, and we can feel proud that such a figure of great wit and wisdom presided over its renaissance. Not only did he point to the true antiquity and usage of the stone circles, but within the tradition of the Order it is said that he 'knew all about the Mount Haemus Grove of 1245 and the reports of an earlier Grove at Oxford, where he lived. He determined to revive Mount Haemus, and a group began to wear the robes and to carry out some of the ceremonies'.[11] It is important to note, however, that we have no hard historical evidence to support this claim. In 1694 it is recorded that a young man named John Toland talked to Aubrey about Druids and stone circles. Toland was 24, and Aubrey 65 at the time, and it is intriguing to think that Aubrey might have invited him to a meeting of the Mount Haemus Grove, although we cannot be certain of this.

Toland was born in Londonderry in 1670 and had completed his education in the liberal arts in Glasgow and Edinburgh. He then began a wandering career, staying in England, then in Leyden for two years, and then back in Oxford. He was a prolific writer with an enquiring mind that led him to fall foul of the established church. In 1696 he published *Christianity Not Mysterious* while living in London. The following year he sailed to Ireland to find his book being burned by the common hangman. He returned to England, and continued to write in his indiscreet and provocative style. In 1717 he published the prophecy of St. Malachy of Armagh which tells of future popes and the end of the papacy.

The Order tradition states that it was in this same year, in September, that a meeting was held at the Apple Tree Tavern in Covent Garden with delegates attending from Druidic and Bardic circles in York, London, Oxford, Wales, Cornwall, the Isles of Man and Anglesey, Scotland, Ireland and Brittany. There they founded the Mother Grove, the *An Tigh Geatha Gairdeachas*[12], thereby founding the modern Druid Order. It was at this meeting that John Toland was apparently elected chosen Chief. The inauguration was announced at the Autumnal Equinox of the same year on Primrose Hill.

In 1720 he was living in Putney and published his *Pantheisticon*, a description of 'natural religion' in a Socratic Society, taking the form of lessons, responses, a canon of philosophy and a litany. In 1722 he died, and it was four years later, in 1726 that his *History of the Druids* was published. Originally he had intended a larger work, but this had never been accomplished, so that his history remains a set of three letters to Lord Molesworth together with appendices.

To some, it seems absurd to suggest that Toland founded the Order. He believed in a personal and direct experience of Christianity and was violently against the abuses of what he termed 'priestcraft' – the manipulation of religion for personal and political ends. In his first letter he tells Lord Molesworth: 'In the mean time I do assure you, My Lord, from all authors, that no Heathen Priesthood ever came up to the perfection of the Druidical, which was far more exquisite than any other such system; as having been much better calculated to beget ingnorance, and an implicit disposition in the people, no less than to procure power and profit to the priests, which is one grand difference between the true worship and the false.' He saw their power over the nobles and the general populace as dangerous: drawing on classical sources he told Lord Molesworth of their 'intolerable power' to wage war or make dishonourable peace; they had the 'address to get themselves exempted from bearing arms, paying taxes or contributing anything to the public but charms'; they were familiar with the arts of Sophistry and juggling and were 'masters of both, and withal to learn the art of managing the mob, which is vulgarly called leading the people by the nose.'

To further cast doubt on the likelihood of his founding the Order is his account of his meeting with Aubrey: 'John Aubrey Esq; a Member of the Royal Society, with whom I became acquainted at Oxford, when I was a sojourner there . . . was the only person I ever then met, who had a right notion of the Temples of the Druids, or indeed any notion that the Circles so often mention'd were such Temples at all: wherein he was intirely confirm'd, by the authorities which I show'd him; as he supply'd me in return with numerous instances of such Monuments, which he was at great pains to observe and set down. And tho' he was extremely superstitious, or seem'd to be so: yet he was a very honest man, and most accurate in his accounts of matters of fact. But the facts he knew, not the reflections he made, were what I wanted.'

Either he was dissembling when writing his history to avoid accusations of being a pagan or Druid, as the previous Chief of the Order Ross Nichols believed, or he was being quite open about his views. If we take his words at face value, it seems highly unlikely that he and Aubrey worked ceremonies together and that he was elected Chosen Chief of the Druid Order. But we must remember that he had experienced the repression of the Church, and that he may well have enjoyed dissembling – letting those who had eyes to see find his true sympathies behind the polemic. His book is filled with fascinating insights into Druidry, and it is perhaps fitting that we should be as uncertain about the foundation of the modern Order as we are about its antecedents. Just as a tree is rooted in darkness, so too is the origin of many spiritual movements, religions and occult groups. It is as if we are forced by contradictory or insufficient historical data to look beyond them to the supernal impulses which guide their births, deaths and rebirths.

John Aubrey's ideas on stone circles influenced another man, William Stukeley. Born in 1687, Stukeley, a young Lincolnshire doctor, had found himself drawn to Stonehenge after seeing engravings of the site. He then read and made notes from a transcript of Aubrey's *Monumenta Britannicum*, and a few years later, in 1719, he visited Stonehenge for the first time. For the next five years he made annual visits to Wiltshire, carrying out a detailed study of both Avebury and Stonehenge which laid the foundations for the development of the modern science of archaeology. The Order's tradition states that Stukeley became the second Chosen Chief of the modern cycle, to be succeeded by such figures as David Samwell, a medical naval officer who travelled with Captain Cook on *Resolution* and *Discovery*, and who wrote the first-hand account of Cook's death at the hands of natives in Hawaii; William Blake, whose remarkable drawings of Avebury and Stonehenge were strongly influenced by Stukeley and who refused to take the oath at his trial at Chichester Assizes, declaring that he was a Druid; Godfrey Higgins, author of three hefty volumes, the first of which was entitled *Celtic Druids*; Gerald Massey who was similarly productive, and who, along with Higgins, was used as source material by Mme Blavatsky; George Watson MacGregor-Reid, who invented the famous health product *Sanatogen* and who stood for both the House of Commons and the American Senate; and Ross Nichols whose *Book of Druidry* has recently been posthumously published.

There is some doubt as to whether Stukeley and Blake really were Druid Chiefs in the way we conceive this term, but little doubt surrounds the other characters in this unusual chain of succession that runs from the eighteenth century to this day. Biographies of each them, including those not mentioned here, are to be found in *The Book of Druidry*.

While these figures guided English Druidry, Welsh Druidry was strongly influenced by a Glamorganshire stonemason, Edward Williams, who took the bardic name Iolo Morganwg. In the late eighteenth century, Morganwg created items of Welsh bardic tradition, based partly or apparently on records, both oral and written, which have since disappeared. Contemporary religious preoccupations combined with his own creative imagination and whatever ancient wisdom records he had inherited to produce a series of literary forgeries which for many years were considered genuine, and resulted in the inclusion of Iolo's Gorsedd ceremony in the perfectly genuine Eisteddfod.

Stuart Piggott, writing in *The Druids*, dismisses all of Iolo's work as fraudulent, but what most writers on these subjects, including Piggott, have failed to understand is that when it comes to working with the esoteric, we are to large extent under the influence of Mercury, or Lugh, the god of communication between the human and divine worlds – the god of what is now becoming known as channelling. But Mercury is also the god of thieves and of deception – of stage magic, and the manipulation of illusion as well as of high magic – the manipulation of consciousness and the causal world. Those who have not clarified their relationship with Mercury, fall prey to both aspects of his influence, and it is then hard for the academic to understand how the same person can combine genuine material with the fraudulent, how they can channel both divinely inspired insights into Druidry and complete nonsense – how they can be upright and honest and engage in deception or delusion.

Whether we consider Iolo's influence an inspiration or a pollution, we know that he contributed towards a revival of the bardic tradition in Wales that lives to this day.

While Welsh and English Druidry were transmitted to the present day in a formal way through the various 'Orders', we must remember that the traditions were also transmitted in a less structured form, in the ways outlined at the beginning of this chapter, through both individuals and groups in these countries and in Ireland, Scotland and Brittany.

EXERCISE – 2

Having read this chapter, spend a few moments forgetting all that you have read, make yourself comfortable, and allow yourself to come to a sense of inner centredness and calm. Let all disturbing thoughts be laid aside. Close your eyes, and focus for a few moments on your breathing. Become aware of the sun rising. Feel yourself bathed in light and warmth. Become this light and warmth if it feels right. Now open your eyes and read this passage, allowing your creative imagination to build the images as you learn of them:

Imagine that you are living in Britain in the seventeenth century. A friend hands you copies of the classical authors' writings on Druidry. That evening, by candlelight you read Caesar, Strabo, Diodorus Siculus, and others, telling of the Druids and of their meetings in

Groves. That night you dream that you have travelled back in time and are consulting with a Druidess or Druid in a sacred Grove. You are given helpful and inspiring guidance.

The following day, you remember that near where you live is a stone circle, perhaps Avebury or Stonehenge. You pack food and drink, mount your horse and ride there with a companion. You find local farmers trying to break up the stones. You talk with them, persuading them that the circle represents a part of their heritage. They leave. You walk amongst the stones, touching them and admiring their simple power and beauty.

Evening falls, and as the stars begin to shine above you, you spend the warm summer night sitting amongst the stones. With your companion you resolve to form a society to research the meaning of these sacred places, and you decide to make a journey soon to the Bards of Wales to see if you might learn more of the Druids and their lore from them. For a moment you fall asleep, and in your sleep a Druid comes to you to say, 'We are always here. Watching and waiting. We will guide and counsel and protect you. The ancient wisdom was known to us in the past and it can be known again. The stars speak through the stones. Light shines in the densest matter. Earth and heaven are one. Our physical beings and our heavenly souls are united in the Mystery of Being.'

You wake up amongst the stones. You return home with your companion on horseback. You see yourself looking in the candlelight at the manuscripts given to you by your friend. You become aware of looking at this book now. You feel yourself fully present in your physical body, here and now filled with vitality and health.

3 · WHO ARE DRUIDS NOW?

In our postcritical naiveté we are now in a period when we become capable once again of experiencing the immediacy of life, the entrancing presence to the natural phenomena about us.

Thomas Berry – *The Dream of the Earth*

Having surveyed both the recent and the ancient past of Druidry, we come to the present day. Who are Druids now? Who is motivated to study Druidry and to practice its ways in this modern age?

My first encounter with a Druid was when I was a child. At about the age of eleven my father, who is a historian, introduced me to a fellow historian and Chief of the Order of Bards, Ovates and Druids, Philip Ross Nichols. I and a friend interviewed him about Stonehenge and Druidry for a magazine we were running. My memories of this meeting are vague, but I remember feeling at ease with this man who rummaged amongst papers to show us charts and diagrams of the monuments. Three years later I met him again, at a time when I had become fascinated by photography. He too was a keen photographer, and during our conversation he invited me to photograph the ceremonies. And so began my encounter with Druidry. Every six weeks or so I would travel to Parliament Hill in Highgate or to the Alliance Hall in Victoria to photograph these ceremonies which increasingly I wanted to participate in, rather than photograph.

When I visited Ross, or Nuinn [Irish for the Ash tree] as he was known in the Order, we would begin our meetings with poring over proofs of the photographs I had taken, often drinking tea and eating sandwiches. But we would soon move on to talking about Druidry and the esoteric. After a few months photography was dispensed with, and our meetings were concerned solely with matters spiritual. I had been drawn to Buddhism when I was eleven or twelve and by the age of fifteen was keen to know all I could of esoteric lore. Nuinn, now in his sixties, had spent all his adult life studying the occult and being a historian he seemed able to retain the sort of detail which my mind struggled to remember. He was particularly fond of scribbling little notes and diagrams on the backs of envelopes or on napkins when we met in a café near his office in Gloucester Road. He was the Principal of a 'crammer's' – a college that specialised in cramming information into students who had failed their exams. At Carlisle and Gregson's or 'Jimmy's' as it was called, there was no sport, no assembly, no distraction from the serious business of fact-stuffing and exam taking. It was to Jimmy's that Winston Churchill [also a Druid] was sent, after failing his exams at Harrow.

We would sometimes hold grove meetings in a classroom or in the staff common room when the building had emptied for the evening. Ross made no secret of his connection with Druidry. His secretary at Jimmy's seemed to spend most of her time typing Order correspondence or teaching material. Occasionally a member of staff or student would be intrigued enough to come to one of the public lectures he organised, or to attend one of the public ceremonies.

Working as a college principal, he was used to teaching and to coaching individual pupils, and this is really what he did with me. We hardly ever talked personally. By that I mean that the content of our discussions never revolved around our personal lives. This sounds strange in retrospect, particularly for me since I have trained in psychotherapy which deals constantly with the personal, and it is hard now to imagine a relationship which has little discussion of the personal. But what it meant was that each time we met we got straight down to business. And our business was Druidry and a study of the occult. I would arrive at his house several times a week after school, and he would just say hello, put the kettle on, and perhaps offer a rather dry sandwich left over from earlier times, or on occasion would cook something – he once gave me a cooking lesson, showing me how to make a nut rissole from scratch. The kettle would boil, he would make two cups of tea, and we would move from the kitchen to an adjacent room which was used for ceremonies and as an overflow classroom for the college a mile away. He would then take one of the teaching discourses of the Order and read it out to me. Having done this, he would begin again at the beginning, picking out the important points, and expanding on related themes. He might then jot a diagram down to clarify the subject, and might conclude by talking about the Order in one way or another. I would then leave, having been mostly silent, but having asked any questions when I felt things weren't clear for me.

After a certain amount of time I asked to be initiated into the Order. My horoscope was cast and the other members of the Triad [the three Guardians of the Order, Chief, Pendragon and Scribe] were consulted. I was initiated on Glastonbury Tor, that Beltane, to the accompaniment of music by the Third Ear band.

Once a fortnight Nuinn held an open meditation group, and half a dozen or so people would come. Some were members of the Order, some were not. After giving a guided meditation, he would meticulously note down the experience of each member of the group, and make remarks when he felt they would be helpful or when he saw connections between the different experiences. He was particularly interested in the way experiences in a group meditation are often related to the position in which one sits in a circle, and the way related positions reflect similar experiences. Often he would ask his secretary to type out the notes he made and would distribute them at the next meeting. He would sometimes draw lines between those positions in the circle which seemed to have connections.

Nuinn wasn't a guru and made no effort to be considered as one. His failings and his humanity were as clearly visible as his capacities and talents. He had the breadth of knowledge of a man who had spent his life in academic and esoteric work, free from the constraints of rearing a family. But that freedom and independence had left its mark, and there was a certain loneliness about him. He had no television, and was eminently capable of busying himself with study and research, but he occasionally displayed the sort of crotchety ill-humour that is often characteristic of old people who live on their own. But on the whole one of his warmest characteristics was the way in which he praised, and in my opinion grossly over-estimated, everybody's talents and abilities. Everyone he knew was very accomplished at something – either he was immensely naive or he was applying one of the prime tenets of the positive thought movement, and seeing people for what they could be rather than simply for what they were.

In his time he had had a fair number of knocks – he earned the distinction of being punched in public on the rostrum of a Poetry

Society meeting by the South African poet Roy Campbell. Ross was chairing the meeting of readings by W. H. Auden and Cecil Day Lewis. Campbell found their poetry insufficiently macho and robust and Ross made the mistake of asking Campbell to stop interrupting.

Ross' disapproval of the mishandling of the election for a new Chief on the death of Robert MacGregor Reid, led him to create a reformed working of the Order with a group of senior Druids, and this decision created an immense bitterness that still lingers in some quarters today. Added to this, Jimmy's always appeared to be going through some crisis or another, either with money or staff or students. In the occult realm, he had brushes with several black magicians, and about these I am glad to say we talked at length. It seems that many of us must go through, at some stage in our esoteric development, encounters with those misguided souls who attempt to use their knowledge for selfish or evil purposes. But despite these difficulties, he was able to travel extensively: of those journeys that I know of, he visited Egypt, Lebanon, Israel, Jordan and Morocco, Greece and Bulgaria, Malta and France, Ireland and the Outer Hebrides. On each of these visits he made sketches, took photographs, and made endless notes, some of which he turned into witty and scholarly journals.

He had met many of the famous figures in the occult establishment of his day – Gerald Gardner and Alex Sanders, J. G. Bennett and Idries Shah, amongst others whose names I have forgotten. But he always kept his own counsel. He enjoyed meeting people, and bringing them together. Nowadays we would call him a 'networker'. He held parties in his house, often before a ceremony such as Imbolc or Samhuinn, which were private by-invitation-only ceremonies. There I met many exciting and eccentric people, not the least of whom was Olivia Robertson, who invited me to stay at her castle in Ireland, and who has now created with her brother, Lawrence, probably the largest and most creative goddess-centred movement in the world.[1]

I spent a hot idyllic summer at the castle, during two weeks of which Nuinn came over, and it was during that time that we had the opportunity to discuss every aspect of the Order and Druidry, without the usual constraints of having to journey home on the underground to prepare for school the next day. It was also wonderful to be free to walk through the thousand-year-old cloister of yew trees to the sacred grove beyond and to feel the purity and ancient power of Ireland breathing through the trees around us as we meditated.

Besides leading the Order, Ross managed to pursue a career as a poet. Three books of his poetry were published, and a new selection of his work chosen and introduced by the contemporary poet Jay Ramsay is due to be published shortly.[2] He contributed many articles on Druidry, the occult and exoteric history to such journals as the *Occult Review* and my father's magazine, *Past and Future*. In 1952 the Forge Press published a twin volume edition of Paul Christian's eighteenth-century French work, *The History of Magic*, which Ross had edited and had combined with articles by friends on astrology and palmistry. Later this edition was pirated by an American publisher, to his impotent distaste, for the cost of legal action was prohibitive. As if this were not enough for one lifetime, Nuinn was also an accomplished water-colourist, to the extent that some of his work was exhibited at the Royal Academy.

To create a place of refuge, where he could be close to nature and where he could paint and write without the distractions of the city, he bought a piece of woodland in Oxfordshire. There he placed two huts, one for himself and one for guests. Furnished simply with camp beds and cooking pots, he was able to live in utter simplicity. He was a follower of the Naturist movement, and there in the privacy of the woods he was able to feel that contact with nature that comes when we free ourselves of all trappings – both psychic and physical. He was able to gather wood, cook over an open fire, and nourish himself with the power of the trees and the stars before returning to his work as Order Chief and college principal, historian, artist and poet.

I have painted this picture of my Druid teacher in some detail because I want to convey the qualities of a modern Druid, and he was a fine example. He was able to combine strong artistic abilities with an enquiring logical mind. He enjoyed working with ceremonial and being in close contact with nature. His viewpoint was eclectic, not limited – he was always studying, to the very end of his life – whether it was the Qabala or Wicca or Sufism. But he always remained a Christian and was a regular visitor to his local church. He was also an ordained deacon in the Celtic Church. During the sixties, the time of Flower Power, he tried his best to understand what was happening with the young in Britain. The psychedelic review *The International Times* published an article of his on William Blake, and he knew both Kathleen Raine and John Michell who were, and still are, leading figures in the worlds of Blakeian studies and astro-archaeology respectively. In the last two years of his life he spent his time writing about Druidry. The resulting *Book of Druidry* was published by the Aquarian Press in 1990.

OTHER MODERN DRUIDS

What of other modern Druids? Of these I can say less, because my relationship with them was less intense. There was Colin Murray, an architect and designer, whom I first met on a coach visit we made to Glastonbury for the Beltane ceremony – a visit I remember well for Nuinn died unexpectedly a few days before this journey. He founded the Golden Section Order, and for a number of years produced *The New Celtic Review*, a fascinating collection of articles and artwork that centred around Druidry and related topics. Colin produced a set of Ogham cards, and I remember him giving me a reading with these exquisite hand-coloured cards in his Chiswick home – filled with Art Nouveau ornaments and a bardic chair from the Cornish Eisteddfod. After his death, his wife Liz continued his work, and the card set has now been published by Rider & Co.

Vera Chapman is another figure whose Druidry inspired her creativity. Now in her nineties and still writing, she was the Scribe of the Triad, and this was an appropriate office, for she has written over a dozen books for both adults and children, many of which draw on her inner knowledge of Druid lore. It was Vera who founded the Tolkien Society in appreciation of Tolkien's contribution to literature, and to the life of the imagination.

Dr. Thomas Maughan who was elected Chief after MacGregor Reid's death was also a creative figure. He, together with a colleague John Damonte, initiated the training of lay homoeopaths in England. Without their pioneering work, the practice of homoeopathy might still be limited to a handful of general practitioners. It is for this reason that one finds many a homoeopath today who practises Druidry.

The psychiatrist Dr. Graham Howe was also a practising Druid, who used to hold ceremonies in his barn in Wales. His ten books, including *She and Me* have been followed in print by *The Mind of the Druid*, an unusual book, which gives both psychological and philosophical insights into the practice of Druidry.

Winston Churchill, as mentioned previously, was initiated into the Albion Lodge of the Ancient and Archaeological Order of Druids in 1908 and Stuart Piggot's book *The Druids* has an amusing photograph of young Winston surrounded by fellow-Druids sporting false beards.

The Order of Bards, Ovates and Druids has the post of Presider, which is fulfilled by a literary figure who is a member of, or sympathetic to, the Order. Lewis Spence, author of *The Mysteries of Britain* and numerous other books on mythology, was Presider as was Charles Cammell, poet and editor of the *Connoisseur* magazine in the 50s. Robert Armstrong, the Secretary of the Poetry Society was Presider when I joined the Order, and the authors John and Caitlín Matthews now hold joint office in this post.

But modern Druids are not all literary figures, doctors, famous prime ministers or psychiatrists. It is true that amongst Druids today we would find doctors, psychoanalysts, healers, poets, artists and musicians, but just as both sexes are equally represented, so are all vocations and ranges of age and interests. It seems that Druidry appeals to many types of people, regardless of race, nationality, education, artistic ability or gender. Druids today are men and women, Dutch and Irish, American and Swedish, unemployed and employed, young and old.

What attracts someone today to Druidry is what has attracted people to all forms of mystery school throughout the ages – the search for greater understanding, for deeper experience and for communion with the god/dess within. As the petro-chemical age collapses around us, we turn to the nourishment and support of the age-old ways which teach that we are not separate from nature but a part of it.

The English attitude to Druidry is intriguing and highly indicative of the national character. On the one hand the English are proud of their traditions, and Druidry is one of them. It was to Britain that continental Druids were sent for 'polishing' before returning to their country, and it is a matter of some pride that an ancient and sophisticated tradition flourished here long before the coming of the Romans. The English would no sooner relinquish the figure of the Druid as part of their national heritage, than they would relinquish Christmas pudding, the Royal family, football or fish and chips. They also undoubtedly take a secret delight in the whackiness of Druidry – the English are renowned for their eccentrics.

But at the same time as this fond regard for a basic element in their heritage, they display the extraordinary philistinism that is unfortunately also one of their characteristics. Just as they openly consider building a military museum by the Stonehenge car-park, or of building over the Rose theatre foundations in London, drunken louts take the opportunity to mock and jeer at Stonehenge ceremonies and the authorities, for their part, take the opportunity to ban all ceremonies there – rejecting comprehensive plans put forward by the Council of British Druid Orders to create a National Eisteddfod at Stonehenge which could become as successful as the Welsh National Eisteddfod held each summer.

Although we might find some of the English unappreciative of their cultural heritage, little of such philistinism exists in the more Celtic countries of Scotland, Ireland and Wales, where they are by nature closer to the heart of the Druid spirit. Druidry is not confined to the British Isles. In France there are numerous Druid Orders and societies, particularly in Brittany, and there are probably more modern-day Druids in France than in Britain.

The English and Welsh Druids have tended towards the serious. Some of the ceremonies of the Ancient Order of Druids and the Ancient Druid Order as practised at Stonehenge and Primrose Hill can be pretty grim affairs. But in the United States there is a healthy current of pagan activity that is working with the power of humour – actively engaging the silliness and absurdity in spiritual and religious practices and using it, rather than pretending it doesn't exist. A number of pagan groups in America started life as jokes, and when the members of the groups found they were getting something out of their activities, they developed in more 'serious' directions.

AMERICAN DRUIDRY

Such was the origin of the Reformed Druids of North America, which began in 1963 as a humorous protest movement against a regulation at Carleton College that required all students to attend a certain number of chapel services. Since students could avoid the requirement by attending services of their own religion, the RDNA held services which were, no doubt, a little livelier than those taking place in the chapel. Although the rule was abolished only a year later, the original founders were horrified to find that the RDNA continued to hold services and spread its organisation far beyond the campus. The joke had become for real. By the mid-seventies the RDNA had spread across seven states, with groves which celebrated the eight festivals, and held outdoor rituals and celebrations. As is the normal pattern, other groups differed in inclination from the RDNA and formed new groups – the NRDNA [New Reformed Druids of North America] include, or used to include, such groups as the Norse Druids in San Diego, Zen Druids in Olympia, Wiccan Druids in Minneapolis, Irish Druids in San Francisco, Hassidic Druids in St.Louis and Eclectic Druids elsewhere.

Margot Adler, in her excellent survey of American Paganism *Drawing Down the Moon*, articulates her understanding of how a group which starts as a joke can develop into one which satisfies the members' spiritual needs: 'When one combines a process of inquiry with content of beauty and antiquity, when, even as a lark, one opens the flow of archetypal images contained in the history and legends of people long negated by this culture, many who confront these images are going to take to them and begin a journey unimagined by those who started the process.' By the mid-eighties, two other Druid groups were in evidence in America: Ar nDraiocht Fein [Our Own Druidism] and Keltria. Ar nDraiocht Fein publishes a journal The Druid's Progress and is particularly keen on researching the links between Middle European, East European and Russian traditions and Druidry. Keltria is as yet a small group, but publishes its own journal and has also begun to create a correspondence course.

American Druidry can help us to see that the value of Druidry does not depend on claiming some unique succession or authoritative position, but on its ability to connect to the spirit of the living Druid Tradition that exists regardless of form or structure. The American Druid groups make no claims to be ancient but they feed from the same source as European groups old and new. Writers like Starhawk[3] and Margot Adler have helped us to see the folly of clinging to rigid structures – ideas of relative authenticity or of supposed succession. They have helped Wiccans to release the energy they bound up in concern over whether Gardnerian or Alexandrian craft was preferable, and indeed how much of the craft had recently been invented, so that this energy could be used for joyful celebration and practical action in the ecological and political arena. American Druidry can teach the Europeans to similarly let go of their obsession with the details of history and authenticity, and instead connect to the inner spirit which is forever living and changing.

Another contribution of American Druidry is that of openly recognising Druidry's ability to be eclectic and to marry with other traditions. The Hassidic Druids, for example, are mainly made up of former Jews who want to keep certain aspects of Hebrew culture but who want to avoid the oppressive nature of its patriarchal theology. They add Yiddish and Hebrew sources to the Gaulish and Celtic ones. They have a set of additional scriptures called the Mishmash, which satirise in a good natured way the Talmud. Margot Adler, herself both pagan and Jewish, finds most of the Mishmash both humorous and profound.

How can one be a Zen Druid? Druidry has a strong Zen streak within it. Dr Graham Howe's fellow psychiatrist R. D. Laing said of his work 'his writing is existential and is Zen.' And what could be more Zen than the massive gateways of Stonehenge? Many Druids are able to combine their Druid practice and understanding with

Christianity or with Wicca, with Native American observances or with Buddhism. Druidry enhances our appreciation of other ways, rather than diminishing it. It creates bridges, not barriers.

It is exciting to find that others appreciate this – the Christians who meet each year at the Conference on Christianity and Druidry, the Wiccans who join in Druid ceremonies and workshops or who meet with Druids at the annual Pagan Federation Conference, and the practitioners of the Native American tradition we meet in America, Holland and England. Such understanding is moving and gives birth to creative partnerships and exciting projects.

There are always a few people and groups who are sectarian and are unable to see beyond their own self-created barriers – the more extreme Christian groups who are terrified of the word 'pagan', even though it simply means a country-dweller, or who are frightened of the connection that paganism has with the earth and with the sky, and are sincerely worried at the apparent absence of Jesus in the pagan scheme, being unaware of the importance of the Christ-Child in Druidry, inherent in the concept of the Mabon, the Divine Child who lives within each of us. Even within Druidry it would be foolish to pretend that all is harmony. Sadly even amongst Druids one finds separatism, sectarianism and sexism: one Druid group who feels an affinity with Wicca will not attend the Conference of Christians and Druids, because they feel that too much cruelty has been inflicted by Christians on Wiccans over the last two thousand years to justify dialogue. Another group will not attend this Conference or join the Council of British Druid Orders because it refuses to recognise the validity of other Druid groups. The largest Druid group denies its female members the right to meet in the same lodges as its male members.[4]

It seems that building barriers is easier than building bridges. Opening to others is often painful. If we have a choice between talking and relating to each other or of fighting or fleeing it is perhaps natural that many should choose to fight or flee rather than to meet. Every religion, native tradition, method of psychotherapy or school of thought seems to fragment and develop separate units which feud or go their own separate ways. It seems to be a natural process. For this reason, rather than bemoaning the state of affairs that we find amongst Druid groups, I prefer to see them as facets of one jewel, segments of one mandala. Each one has something to offer, something that can help someone at some time in their life.

The groups with a public face existing in Britain at the present are as follows:

The Ancient Order of Druids

With over 3000 members this is the largest Druid organisation in Britain. Founded by Henry Hurle in 1781, its purposes are primarily charitable and social, and they have done wonderful work in fund-raising for children in need and the disabled. They celebrate certain ceremonies, but do not have any teaching programme. They are organised in lodges, most of which are male-only. There are a few female-only lodges. Found mainly in the South and West of England, the organisation has affinities with masonry in its chains of office and aspects of its ceremony, and affinities with the Rotary Club in its social and fund-raising bias.

The United Ancient Order of Druids

A breakaway movement from the Ancient Order, formed in 1833, they are primarily a Friendly Society, and have lodges worldwide.

The Glastonbury Order of Druids

They were formed in 1988. Small but articulate, their concern is primarily with Stonehenge and the Glastonbury mythos.

The Secular Order of Druids

Formed in 1986, this group is particularly concerned with working within the landscape and with promoting a National Eisteddfod at Stonehenge. In 1975 their Chief formed a support group for the Druids which he felt were being squeezed out of Stonehenge by the rock festival, and ten years later he formed the Order and wrote new, progressive ceremonies aimed at the young.

The Universal Druid Order

A small group formed in 1988 with an authority deriving from W. B. Crow the well-known occult writer, their main interest is in performing the four solar ceremonies each year at Conway Hall in London. Their concern is primarily with the power of ritual to effect healing and changes in consciousness.

The Ancient Druid Order

This group is sometimes abbreviated to The Druid Order, although this is a generic name which any Order might use in a subsidiary sense. They perform the Summer Solstice at Stonehenge, when allowed by the police, the Spring Equinox at Tower Hill and the Autumnal Equinox at Primrose Hill. Although this is the most photographed group, since it has, until recently, used Stonehenge for its annual solstice ceremony, it now represents the 'rump' of the old Order, said traditionally to have been founded in 1717, out of which the Order of Bards, Ovates and Druids developed.

The College of Druidism in Edinburgh

Run by the colourful and bombastic Kaledon Naddair who issues quantities of booklets, posters, incenses and jewellery relating to the type of Druidry that he describes as Keltic and Pictish shamanism.

The Order of Bards, Ovates and Druids

A development of the Ancient Druid Order, founded in 1717, the OBOD was constituted in 1964 and is now one of the largest Druid groups. Working to awaken Druidry from within, with a teaching programme that relates environmental and artistic concerns with spiritual ones, it promotes equality of the sexes and encourages the development of autonomous groups. It runs a postal course, and holds workshops and regular retreats.

The Welsh, Breton and Cornish Druid groups

These are fundamentally cultural rather than esoteric groups. They are usually made up of native speakers who have a great love of their national culture, which they seek to foster and preserve through the holding of annual Eisteddfodau [the plural of Eisteddfod, which literally means 'A Festival of Listening']. These events usually take place outdoors in the summer and include numerous stalls, as at a village fair, Gorsedd ceremonies with fully robed participants, poetry and music recitals, and the giving of prizes. Although able to trace their foundations far back, well beyond AD 950 in the case of the Welsh, the formal organisation of annual Eisteddfodau is a recent phenomenon, occurring from 1860 in Wales, 1899 in Brittany and 1928 in Cornwall.

Each of the groups listed is unique and attracts a different type of person. Seeing these widely differing groups as aspects of one Mandala helps us to sense how they relate to each other. Into the segment of the Mandala that is concerned with promoting the

Arts, fall the Welsh, Cornish and Breton Druid groups who hold their annual *Eisteddfodau*. Into the segment that is concerned with engaging in charitable work falls the Ancient Order of Druids, with its 3000 members. Into the segment that is engaged with promoting our freedom to worship at Stonehenge and to foster an appreciation of Sacred Landscape fall the Glastonbury Order of Druids and the Secular Order of Druids. Into the segment that is concerned with celebrating the solar festivals of the equinoxes and solstices as a spiritual and ceremonial work fall the Universal Druid Order and the Ancient Druid Order. And into the section that is concerned primarily with teaching Druidry to a wider public, fall the College of Druidism in Edinburgh and the Order of Bards, Ovates and Druids.

This way of grouping and arranging the various Druid Orders has its limitations – it should be understood that each group engages in several functions, the categories simply indicating their most prominent function – and I have not included the many groups in France for reasons of space and lack of full knowledge. There are also autonomous groups working in these islands and elsewhere who have no public face and therefore about whom nothing can be said in this context, since their activities remain private.

EXERCISE – 3

Having read this chapter, spend a few moments forgetting all that you have read, making yourself comfortable, and allowing yourself to come to a sense of inner centredness and calm. Let all disturbing thoughts be laid aside. Close your eyes, and focus for a few moments on your breathing. Become aware of the sun rising. Feel yourself bathed in light and warmth. Become this light and warmth if it feels right. Now open your eyes and read this passage, allowing your creative imagination to build the images as you learn of them:

Imagine that a friend invites you to a Druid ceremony. You are intrigued and amused. 'Do Druids still exist?', you ask your friend. He or she suggests you find out by coming along. You experience some anxiety as you travel to the house of a Druid in the country. You feel that you might be about to meet some very odd characters. You are relieved to find a group of people who seem in many ways unremarkable in their ordinariness – their 'everydayness'. After chatting briefly, you leave the house to gather in a small grove in the woods near to the house. Almost imperceptibly the 'everydayness' of the people and the surroundings changes. One by one each person steps into the sacred circle. Now it is your turn. As you step forward,

41

you feel its strength and its power, its sacredness and its protection. The ceremony begins and you find it inspiring, calming, moving.

When it is over, it is your turn to step out of the circle. As you do so, you feel yourself returning to the everyday world. But somehow it is different. You look at your friend, at the others. You realise that they are, and they are not, Druids. You realise it is a label like any other, which is used only for convenience, for we need words to communicate and to define. You become aware of holding this book in your hands, and of yourself here and now, before standing up and stretching.

4 · BARDS, OVATES AND DRUIDS

Among all the Gallic peoples, generally speaking, there are three sets of men who are held in exceptional honour: the Bards, the Vates, and the Druids. The Bards are singers and poets; the Vates, diviners and natural philosophers; while the Druids, in addition to natural philosophy, study also moral philosophy.

Strabo – *Geographica* (written at the end of the first century BC)

The Druids organised themselves into three distinct groupings, in which each group had specific functions and tasks to perform, and a specific training. Fortunately, the classical texts give sufficient information to enable us to form a picture of the nature of each of these groupings, and once we have done this we can then consider their relevance in contemporary Druid training.

BARDS

And there are among them composers of verses whom they call Bards; these singing to instruments similar to a lyre, applaud some, while they vituperate others.

Diodorus Siculus – (*Histories*) 8 BC

The Bards were the keepers of tradition, of the memory of the tribe – they were the custodians of the sacredness of the Word. Although they represented the first level of training for an apprentice Druid, we should not make the mistake of thinking that a Bard was

43

somehow in a lowly or inferior position. There were many levels of accomplishment, but the most skilled of Bards were held in high esteem and partook of many of the functions of both the Ovate and the Druid.

The training of a Bard was intense and lasted for many years. There were variations in the curricula between Scotland, Ireland and Wales. In Ireland it is recorded that the training lasted twelve years, with students undergoing the following rigorous curriculum: In his first year, the student progressed from Principle Beginner [*Ollaire*] to Poet's Attendant [*Tamhan*] to Apprentice Satirist [*Drisac*]. During this time he had to learn the basics of the bardic arts: grammar, twenty stories and the Ogham tree-alphabet. Over the next four years, he learnt a further ten stories each year, a hundred ogham combinations, a dozen philosophy lessons, and an unspecified number of poems. He also studied diphthongal combinations, the Law of Privileges and the uses of grammar. By his sixth year the student, if he had stayed the course, was called a Pillar [*Cli*] and would study a further forty-eight poems and twenty more stories. Over the following three years, he was termed a Noble Stream [*Anruth*] because 'a stream of pleasing praise issues from him, and a stream of wealth to him.'[1] During this time he learnt a further ninety-five tales, bringing his repertoire up to 175 stories. He studied prosody, glosses, prophetic invocation, the styles of poetic composition, specific poetic forms, and the place-name stories of Ireland. The final three years of his training entitled him to become an *Ollamh*, or Doctor of Poetry, passing through the grades of Man of Learning [*Eces*] and Poet [*Fili*]. In his tenth year the student had studied further poetic forms and composition, in his eleventh year 100 poems, and in his twelfth year 120 orations and the four arts of poetry. He or she was now the Master or Mistress of 350 stories in all. As *Ollamh*, Doctor of Poetry, he was entitled to receive a gold branch. As *Anruth*, Noble Stream, he had carried a silver branch, and before that, throughout his training, he had carried a bronze branch. These branches had bells attached to them, so that as the poet strode into the hall to recite a poem or tell a tale, he would be accompanied by the sound of bells warning the audience to become silent, and summoning the help of the inner realms to ensoul his poem or story. In Wales and Scotland the training of a bard was similarly rigorous, although with different grades and a different curriculum.

How were the Bards trained? Bardic schools formed around a Chief Poet and his attendants. A good deal of time was spent in learning by rote, to strengthen the memory and learn the fantastic number of tales and poems required of an accomplished bard. Records from both the Western Highlands and Ireland show that much work was undertaken through the technique we would now term sensory deprivation. Their accommodation was spartan in the extreme, and much time would be spent incubating poems and seeking inspiration in total darkness. It is only recently that we have rediscovered, through the pioneering work of Dr John Lilly,[2] the fructive power of the darkness found in the isolation tank.

Their curriculum suggests a rigorous and burdensome acquisition of other people's stories and poems. But this was only part of their work. They were training to become masters of both Record and Inspiration. It was only one of their tasks to record the lore, laws and genealogy of the Tribe. Just as important as performing this task of keeping alive tradition and heritage, they were entrusted with coming to a knowledge of the sacred power of the Word, manifest as the ability to become inspired and to inspire others. To carry the records of the tribe they needed to know the stories and poems which preserved the lineage and the lore of their people, but to be Masters of Inspiration they needed to compose their own poems and tales. It was for this reason that they practised sensory deprivation, and employed the arts of invocation. Such a training naturally awoke inner powers. A powerful memory, and an ability to plumb the depths and roam the heights of consciousness in search of inspiration and the creative flame, developed within the bard an ability to see into the future and influence the world around him in a way that foreshadowed the work of the Ovate and the Druid, and which allowed him to carry the spirit of Druidry through the centuries when the light of both the Ovate and the Druid could not be seen in the world.

It is fitting that the first grade of Druid training should so encompass the work of both the Ovate and the Druid. It seems that the Druid would concur with the opening words of John: 'In the beginning was the Word'. The way in which the word could create, command, nourish, heal, cut through, purify, invoke, unite, provoke, deter and bind was a power that the Bard in his long training came to know and utilise in the service of himself, his patron, his King, his Druid, and hopefully, his God or Goddess.

> O Hear the voice of the Bard
> Who present, past and future sees
> Whose ears have heard the holy Word
> That walked among the ancient trees . . .
>
> William Blake – *Songs of Experience*

Knowing something of what the Bards did and how they were trained, we can now ask ourselves what relevance the Bardic work might have for us today.

It is no coincidence that we begin our study in Druidry within the Bardic Grade. Its importance as a foundation for our lives and character and spiritual development is no less significant now than it was thousands of years ago, and it could be argued that it is even more essential today than it was then. The clue to understanding why this should be so lies in the realisation that the historical Bards worked with Record and with Inspiration. One of the prime reasons for modern man's sense of alienation lies in the fact that he has cut himself adrift from both the natural world and from the roots of his past. Practising Druidry is about healing this alienation – reconnecting to our past and to the world of nature. In the Bardic grade we open ourselves to the restorative power of the Druid understanding of Nature – we allow the Mandala of the Eightfold Seasonal Cycle, explained in the next chapter, to be grounded in our beings. Working with Record means working with heritage, lineage, and the mythology and stories of the tribe. Working with Inspiration means opening ourselves to our inner creativity.

Many of the problems that we suffer from in the developed world result from our suppression and denial of the artistic, in all its forms. Modern brain research shows that for most of us, our primary mode of functioning comes from the dominant cerebral hemisphere, which mediates the function of analytical thinking. The opposite hemisphere has less of a say in our current way of living – it is the hemisphere that mediates the synthesising, non-analytic forms of thought and expression: it is the part of the brain considered responsible for artistic expression. It is generally agreed that to become complete we need to allow both sides of ourselves adequate opportunities for development and expression. This truth was expressed by the Alchemists (and there is a strong tradition of Alchemy within Druidry) and later by Carl Jung, who developed his theory of the archetypal Logos and Eros – male and female aspects of the psyche which for our development need to relate and eventually or periodically conjoin. Alchemists knew of the importance of this Conjunction, and they termed it the Mystical Marriage or the *Mysterium Coniunctionis*. Now modern brain research has helped us to observe a possible physical correlation of these two aspects of the Self by showing the way that different brain functions are apportioned between the two hemispheres.

Our education has, for the most part, concentrated on developing our skills of analytical and mathematical thinking, although the Steiner schools are noticeable in their attempt to accord equal status to artistic development in their curricula. When we enter the Bardic Way, we begin a process that develops our less dominant hemisphere. We open ourselves to the artistic, the creative self. This is no simple task, and in a way typical of Druidry, the work is undertaken in an apparently round-about way. Through working with the eightfold festival scheme, and with the power of the four elements that are allocated to the cardinal points in the sacred circle of Druid working, the Bard is brought to a stage where she has acknowledged and worked with the four aspects of her being, – represented by earth, her practicality and sensuality; water, her receptivity and emotionality; air, her reasoning; and fire, her intuition and enthusiasm. These four elements and parts of the Self being accessed, worked with and harmonised, the Bardic aspirant opens to her inner creativity. She then has the resources of her body and heart, mind and intuition available to guide and inspire her. By working in this way, we learn to by-pass the rational mind which so loves to create limits to understanding.

To be able to operate, the intellect creates distinctions, categories, mental constructions, through which experience can be comprehended and acted upon. This is essential for our survival and progress in the world. The problems arise when this ability to create frames of reference is not counter-balanced by the ability to transcend these frames and open ourselves to the trans-rational – the inexplicable-in-words-but-no-less-true. Poetry and music are supremely competent at helping us to go beyond frames and viewpoints. Sound, spoken, sung or played, stretches our boundaries, opens horizons, invokes energies that the intellect alone cannot grasp or categorise with its workings. Here is the power of the Bard – to dissolve our boundaries, our frames of reference – even if only for a moment.

Take this poem, by the modern Bard Jay Ramsay:[3]

> Fathomless unknown,
> Behind and in everything –
> Valley – kestrel – celandine:
> You nowhere, and in everything –
>
> And being nothing, being silenced,
> Being unable to speak
> You see everything,
> And I see You
> And I see I am
> The core I am seeing:
> The sun closening

> To meet the man
> Who has crossed the line,
> Who has walked out of himself
>
> Stands ahead there,
> Naked in the light.

One's mind cannot fully grasp the power of such a poem – one is impacted by the force of the words and imagery in a way that defies description or explanation. This is the work of poetry, of the bard. To go beyond. To travel. To bring back. Professor Michael Harner, a world authority on shamanism, speaks of the shamanic way as one which is best defined as a method to open a door and enter a different reality.[4] This is precisely what happens with powerful and effective poetry. The difference between 'secular' poetry writing, reading and reciting and the same activities undertaken in the spirit of bardism is that in the latter this shamanic process is consciously acknowledged and worked with. Creativity and inspiration are seen as gifts of the Gods, as powers entering the vessel of the Self through the Superconscious. Appropriate preparation, ritual, visualisation, prayer and meditation create the channels through which such generative, creative power can flow.

The relevance of this work to the contemporary artistic scene is clear: when art became secularised what it gained in freedom of expression, it lost in depth of inspiration. Now we have turned full circle and are able to spiritualise our art once again, freed at last from the limitations of religious dogma, and able to transcend the obsession with personal fame and recognition.

The Bardic stream is not simply a body of knowledge we once possessed and which we attempt to regain, it is a spiritualised mode of artistic creative consciousness which is dynamic and living – the future holds as much, if not greater promise than the past. The Bards undoubtedly made music and danced: the stone circles are made for dancing, and the current interest in circle dancing pioneered by Professor Bernard Wosien[5] allows us to reconnect again to the ancient power of the circular communal dance around the still point of the centre. Many spiritual traditions have their particular disciplines of sacred movement: there are, for example, the whirls of the dervishes, Sufi dancing, Tai Ch'i, Paneurythmy,[6] the Gurdjieff movements and Rudolf Steiner's Eurythmy. Recently a system of Druid movement meditation has been uncovered by three Germans,[7] and there are intriguing stories of Druid dances still being practised and remembered on the Continent. It is certainly possible that traces of this early sacred and celebratory dancing is contained within Morris dancing, the Abbot's Bromley Horn dance, and other folk dances. Our challenge is to rediscover the music, chants and dances of the Druids by contacting the archetypal sources of inspiration within. These sources are transpersonal and out-of-time. They fed the Druids in the past and they can feed us now. We know some of the instruments they used: the lyre or harp, a form of horn, with a sound like the Australian aborigine's didgeridoo and almost certainly the bodhran or animal-skin drum and the claves – two sticks of wood banged together to produce a rhythm alone or counterpoised with that of the drum.

Contemporary music and theatre is already drawing on the deep wells of Celtic inspiration. To give just a few examples: Clannad, Enya, Derek Bell of the Chieftains, and the Theatre Taliesin in Wales are all openly working with the spirit of these wells. Jay Ramsay, with the Angels of Fire group of performing poets and their collection of poetry that draws on the spiritual sources of inspiration to be found in the four elements,[8] are yet another example of artists working with the current that we can term 'bardic'. The potential for enhanced creativity is immense when we recontextualise our creativity in terms of the sacred. Previously this involved being bound by Christian themes and dogma. Now it means recognising the sacredness, not only of the Spirit, but of our Earth, of the four elements, and of our generativity and creativity itself.

In the Bardic Grade we open to what it means to be living on the earth with the ability to be creative. Although this is the first stage of Druid training, its purpose reaches to the very heart of Druidry, which is the development of a mastery of the powers of generation. At the Bardic level this involves the generation of creative works – of music, song, poetry and art in all its forms. In the Ovate and Druid work we relate to this power in the same way but we also become concerned with generating healing and love, ideas and light. The Bard's knowledge of and skill with the power of the Word becomes magical with the Druid: understanding the creative force of sound, the Word is used to generate seeds of light that echo through creation.

The tree which represents the Bardic Grade is the Birch – appropriately it is the first tree of the Ogham tree-alphabet, and the tree which represents new beginnings, pioneering and giving birth. The West is the place of the Bard. It is from the West that we enter the circle in our ceremonies, and the West is therefore the place of Entrance, of beginnings – the receptive, feminine West that faces the East of the Dawn Ray. The times associated with the Bardic Grade are the Spring,

49

and Dawn – times when we are fresh and ready to begin a new cycle of learning and experience.

OVATES

To you alone it is given to know the truth about the gods and deities of the sky . . . The innermost groves of far-off forests are your abodes. And it is you who say that the shades of the dead seek not the silent land of Erebus and the pale halls of Pluto; rather, you tell us that the same spirit has a body again elsewhere, and that death, if what you sing is true, is but the mid-point of long life.

Lucan – *Pharsalia* c.60AD

Lucan, in the above quotation, is addressing Druids generally, but it is an appropriate quotation to open our study of the Ovate Grade, for it was the Ovates who, to the greatest degree, were responsible for understanding the mysteries of death and rebirth, for transcending time – for divining the future, for conversing with the Ancestors – travelling beyond the grave to bring augury and counsel to those still living on earth. If the Bards were shamans in Michael Harner's understanding of the term because they opened doors with the power of the Word, then the Ovates deserve to be called shamans even more so, for they open the doors of Time itself. A general categorisation of the three different grades accords the arts to the bards, the skills of prophecy and divination to the Ovates and philosophical, teaching, counselling and judicial tasks to the Druid.

The Ovate as master or mistress of prophecy and divination needed, and still needs today, a reorientation in relation to Time. To travel within time, to read the Akashic Records as some would term it, requires a conception of its nature and dynamics that is radically different to post-Enlightenment thinking, and more akin to the understanding now being offered by the New Physics.

The belief in the cyclicity of life, as we shall see in the next chapter, was fundamental. In common with the Hindus, the Druids believed in reincarnation. Of this item of Druid belief there is no doubt, for it is confirmed many times in the classical sources. Caesar, in *De Bello Gallico* says 'The cardinal doctrine which they seek to teach is that souls do not die, but after death pass from one to another; and this belief, as the fear of death is thereby cast aside, they hold to be the greatest invective to valour.' Diodorus quotes Posidonius when he says that the Druids held that 'the souls of men are immortal, and that after a definite number of years they live a second life when the soul passes to another body.'

50

Now we can understand how the Ovates were able to conceive of time-travel. The Realm of the Ancestors was not the realm of people dead-and-gone, it was the repository of tribal wisdom, the realm in which the Ancestors lived whilst awaiting reincarnation and to which the Ovate could turn for guidance and inspiration on behalf of the tribe.

The experience of the shaman is one in which he undergoes some type of death but returns to life only this time knowing the inner soul-geography. In the past, this experience of returning to life from the realm of death was a rare occurrence. Today, with sophisticated techniques for reviving the body, it is becoming more frequent. A growing academic interest in the subject means that we now have an enormous amount of data on these near-death experiences.[9] Out of the thousands of such experiences recorded a clear pattern emerges: the dying person hears cracking, clicking, or rushing noises, or sometimes wonderfully harmonious sounds; this is followed by an experience of leaving the physical body – observing their physical body and surroundings from a distance; they then feel themselves drawn through a dark tunnel out of which they emerge into brilliant light. This light assumes an almost personal quality and frequently encounters occur with spiritual helpers or protective beings and the Ancestors – friends and relatives who have died previously. There then often follows a rapid review of their life in which they realise instantly where they acted rightly or wrongly. This experience of self-judgement is followed by an entry into a state of being in which past, present and future merge into one reality, a world filled with ecstasy, radiant colours, and immensely beautiful landscapes. We know nothing more, with such certainty, of the post-death state for those who reach this realm of beauty are then brought to a Being who tells them that they must return to their body – their visit, this time, has been only temporary.

What does this tell us of the Ovate work? Firstly that the realm of the Ancestors does exist, and that it can provide succour and guidance. Secondly that a realm exists in which time is transcended, or fundamentally changed. It is to these realms that the shaman travels, to bring back guidance from Past Souls and insights into the future.

In megalithic times the early Druids were probably not distinctively classed into three branches of learning. The Druid shaman would probably have also been the Bard and Ovate, the doctor and priest and repository of tribal lore all in one. The bones found in the chambered cairns such as West Kennet Long Barrow near Avebury would almost certainly have been used ritually in the way bones have been throughout the world, to summon the protection of the dead, to ward off evil and to offer augury.

It is the Ovate's particular connection with the Other World, with death, which makes him the officiant in the rite of Samhuinn – the feast for the departed on 31st October. But it is only in the naive imagination that this concern with death is viewed as morbid, for in reality the Ovate is concerned with new life, with regeneration. She knows that to be born she has to die, whether that means in the literal sense or in the figurative sense which all psychotherapists understand as the essential pre-requisite to change and the healthy development of the psyche.

In working with the processes of death and regeneration, the Ovates' particular study is, fittingly, tree-lore, herbalism and healing. The plant world is a great teacher of the laws of death and rebirth, of sacrifice and transmutation, and the tree is the supreme teacher of the mysteries of time, with its roots for the most part invisible in the past and the subconscious, and its fruit and leaves likewise mostly hidden from us in the heights of the superconscious, holding the potential of the future in the seeds that will in due time fall.

The art of healing concerns the application of natural law to the human body and psyche. If the heart, mind or body is out of tune with nature we suffer. The application of natural remedies, with plants, with the four elements, with solar, lunar and stellar power, are studied by the Ovate. Knowing that it is only through death to one state that we achieve a wider life, the Ovate is in this sense also a psychotherapist. The Ovate learns and teaches that it is only by letting go, rather than holding on, that we truly find what we have been seeking.

How is the Ovate Way of relevance to us today? The fact that many healers, of both body and soul, find Druidry helpful lies in its ability to open the Self to something more than just the personal. Psychotherapy began by discovering the value in opening up communication between the different parts of ourselves (our intrapersonal world). Healing occurred, for example, when our sexual selves were able to relate more openly with our rational cultivated selves; or when our hearts were able to speak freely to our minds. But this was found to be insufficient, for not only do we need to have successful communication between the different parts of ourselves, we also need effective communication with those around us (in our inter-personal relationships). Group therapy was born. More healing occurred as we shared our fears and joys with others, discovering our common humanity and our unique differences. But more was needed – we could resolve a good deal of our intrapersonal and interpersonal difficulties, but we were still haunted by 'existential neurosis' – we needed to move beyond the personal to the transpersonal, to find our place in existence by going beyond the Self. The spiritual psychologies were born. We opened up the channels of communication not only between ourselves and others, but also with our Overself, our Transpersonal Self and with the Divine.

It might be thought that we had covered everything – man had been put back into relationship with himself, with his fellow humans and with his God. But the existential neurosis and sense of alienation in societies and individuals continues because in all this therapy we have been guilty of 'speciesism': we have ignored our relations with the rest of nature. We may have succeful communication with humanity and God, but what about with our home, the Earth? With the stars and sky, with animals and trees? The Druid argument, and the argument of all earth religions or ways, is that we can only be fully healthy, fully whole, physically, psychologically and indeed spiritually, when we have communion with all of nature. The walls of the consulting room and the church collapse ... patient and analyst, confessing and confessor, walk away from the debris, remove their clothes and immerse themselves in the pool that stands before them in the light of the sun. Only then are they whole. Only then can they claim that the healing is complete.

We have an insight into the healing power that Druidry can bring, and the way in which this can be mediated by the Ovate with her knowledge of herb, tree and animal lore and her ability to commune with the spirits of the departed, but what of her divinatory skills?

Understanding the hidden dynamics of Time and knowing the reality of the spirit worlds enables the Ovate to divine without the interference of the rational mind. This mantic work falls into three categories: augury – which is the making of predictions based on signs and omens; divination – which uses particular methods for finding hidden things, whether they be 'intangibles' such as future events or 'tangibles' such as water or metal; and prophecy – which needs no outer methods but which depends on the Ovate's ability to channel higher wisdom in relation to future events.

The methods of augury used in the past were many: from simple weather-witching to sophisticated interpretation of bird flight, from the observation of animal behaviour to the interpretation of planetary configurations. Almost certainly each of the four elements was used for augury, as they were used for healing. The signs and associated feelings conveyed by earth cast on a sheet or drum-skin were read as a modern fortune teller might read the tea-leaves or in Eastern Europe the coffee grounds. The shapes of passing clouds or of the images found in the fire or in gazing into pools of water were further sources of inspiration. It is said that haruspicy was practised by the Druids. This horrendous means of augury was certainly practised by a number of societies in the remote past, including the Etruscan and the Roman. It involved the ritual stabbing of a victim and the careful observation of his death throes – it was the nature and direction of the convulsions and the blood flow which gave augury. Whether classical writers accused the Druids of such rites for purely propaganda purposes or whether they were actually performed we will never know. Many evil and repugnant acts have been carried out in the name of religion, and particularly by Christianity. As difficult as it is to forget these powerful images of cruelty, it is important that we do not let them obscure our appreciation of the supernal values conveyed by those who would have condemned these acts as strongly as we would. We know for certain that under the guise of Christianity monstrous acts of inhumanity were enacted. We cannot know for certain whether this applied to Druidry. My teacher, Nuinn, was convinced that such reports were Roman propaganda to justify their attempts to exterminate the Druids. From the point of view of academic history we can never be sure.

Divination is a more sophisticated form of augury. It is claimed that the Druids used the Ogham or the Coelbren tree-alphabets for divination. We cannot be sure that this is true historically, but they certainly provide us today with evocative means of understanding hidden dynamics and future events. Divination need not be simple fortune-telling – an attempt to see into the future. It can be an effective means of revealing hidden dynamics, whether they be within oneself or within a relationship, or within a group. Divination then becomes a means of gaining self-knowledge and a deeper understanding of the hidden causes behind appearances. Seen in this way it becomes no longer an irreverent attempt to pierce the veil which nature has placed between us and our future, but yet another means to go beyond the surface, to plumb the depths, to look at causes rather than effects. Modern day Ovates are able to turn in this quest to a number of distinctly Druidic methods of divination [see Resources section].

But it is not only the divination of the subtle, intangible realms of the psyche and the future that is the field of Ovate study. Divination can be carried out for tangible things, for water and for metal, for items lost or deliberately hidden, and it is with the wand of hazel that the Ovate divines. Water sources were always accorded special reverence by the Druids – not only were they naturally dependent on a good supply of drinking water, but springs were revered because they demonstrated the source of life springing up out of the body of mother-Earth. The Ovate, with his divining skill would have been used to find water sources and sources of metallic ore, for this was important to the Celts who used both bronze and iron. The Druid, in his capacity as Pheryllt, or Druid Alchemist, worked the metals that the Ovate found for him in a raw state in the earth. And here we perceive another function of the Ovate – to seek out and find what is hidden. It is the Ovate who finds the sacred groves in which the Druids, or the whole Order, works. It is the Ovate who finds the wisdom of the Spirit, plant and animal world and brings it back for the benefit of all. We can surmise that it was the Ovate in this aspect of his work who was responsible for finding criminals and stolen property or missing bodies. The Ovate was the detective as the Druid was the magistrate or judge.

Finally we learn that prophecy was a function of the Ovate. Here the Ovate needed no outer form to help him find what was hidden. His years of training as a Bard then as an Ovate, his ability to commune with the spirits, his refinement of his being and his attunement to the world of nature meant that at certain times he could prophesy, predicting the future or warning of possible dangers so that they could be avoided. Merlin is seen in his Ovate role when he utters the prophecies compiled by Geoffrey of Monmouth in the twelfth century.[10]

The ability to prophesy should be understood in its widest sense within the Ovate work. The Bard learns how to open herself to transpersonal creative energies to provide inspiration and integration. The Ovate builds on this connection with the inner world and combines it with her ability to negotiate time-tracks, so that she can also channel transpersonal creative energies. These channellings may take the form of prophecies, in the sense that they deal with that aspect of time which we term the 'future', or they may deal with hidden levels of reality and causation that require elucidation and communication.

The Ovate curriculum is vast indeed. Just as the Bard needed years of training, so did the Ovate, although we have no details of this from the classical authors. When Druidry went underground, the Bards suffered the least – they simply pretended to be 'mere' minstrels and poets all the while carrying the tradition in their hearts, hidden in their words and music. The Ovates blended into the background, becoming the fortune-tellers and herbalists – keeping the tradition alive through their healing and divinatory work. It was the Druids proper who had the hardest time.

The tree which represents the Ovate Grade is the Yew, the tree of death and rebirth, of eternity. The North is the place of the Ovate, for it is the Grade in which we learn of 'The spiritual intelligence of the night' (*The Book of Taliesin*) when we understand the mystery that the spirit is reborn in the place of greatest darkness. The times associated with the Ovate Grade are Autumn and Winter, evening, dusk and midnight – times when we assimilate the experience of the day or the year, and when we are nourished by the great depths of the Unconscious.

DRUIDS

> Often when the combatants are ranged face to face, and swords are drawn and spears bristling, these men come between the armies and stay the battle, just as wild beasts are sometimes held spellbound. Thus even among the most savage barbarians anger yields to wisdom, and Mars is shamed before the Muses.
>
> Diodorus Siculus – *Histories* circa 8 BC

The reason we tend to visualise the Druid as an old man in our imagination is partly due, perhaps, to a realisation that by the time one has undertaken the training of Bard and Ovate one is bound to be ancient! If it took a dozen years to be a Bard, how much longer must it have taken to learn the skills of Ovate and Druid? We cannot be sure of the exact time it took, but Caesar mentions that it took twenty years to train as a Druid, although Stuart Piggott rightly points out that this could have been a figure of speech to denote a long duration of time, or that it might have actually been 19 years, since the Druids almost certainly used the Meton Cycle, a method of reckoning based on the nineteen-year lunar cycle. It seems that whatever the period was, it included the earlier stages of Bardic and Ovate training.

If the Bard was the poet and musician, the preserver of lore, the inspirer and entertainer, and the Ovate was the doctor, detective, diviner and seer, what was the Druid? His functions, simply stated, were to act as adviser to kings and rulers, as judge, as teacher, and as an authority in matters of worship and ceremony. The picture this paints is of mature wisdom, of official position and privilege, and of roles which involved decision-making, direction and the imparting of knowledge. We tend to think of the Druid as a sort of priest but this is not borne out by the evidence. The classical texts never refer to them as priests, but as philosophers. At first this appears confusing since we know they presided at ceremonies, but if we understand that Druidry was a natural, earth or solar religion as opposed to a revealed religion, such as Christianity or Islam, we can see that they acted not as mediators between God and man, but as directors of ritual, as shamans guiding and containing the rites.

DRUIDS AS JUDGES

> The Druids are considered the most just of men, and on this account they are entrusted with the decision, not only of the private disputes, but of the public disputes as well; so that, in former times, they even arbitrated cases of war and made the opponents stop when they were about to line up for battle, and the murder cases in particular were turned over to them for decision.
>
> Strabo – *Geographica*

> It is they who decide in almost all disputes, public and private; and if any crime has been committed, or murder done, or there is any dispute about succession or boundaries, they also decide it, determining rewards and penalties: if any person or people does not abide by their decision, they ban such from sacrifice, which is their heaviest penalty.
>
> Caesar – *De Bello Gallico*

It has always been the tradition in the Order that the Druids were not responsible for the human sacrifices mentioned by the classical writers. If we take the accounts of the famous wicker men – huge frames of wood made in human shape in which criminals and others were said to have been set ablaze – we shall see that by studying the classical writers' wording carefully we can come to our own assessment of whether or not this occurred.

In the quotation from Caesar given above, he notes that the Druids severest punishment was ostracism. In a highly ordered society one's position, image, standing and reputation were vital. Losing face was, and still is, in many societies, the most terrible punishment. One can see the power that an individual's sense of self had over him even into the nineteenth century in Ireland, in J. M. Synges remarks in the *Aran Islands*, when he notes with astonishment that when a fisherman had done wrong, he took the boat over to Galway alone to put himself in jail. The wound inflicted by ostracism was a soul-wound, not a physical one. It penetrated to the very heart of whom one felt oneself to be in the world. Caesar did not state that the Druids' severest punishment was to be sacrificed or to be burnt, he stated that their most severe punishment involved barring the person deemed guilty from participating in the sacrifices – in

57

other words the religious ceremonies, which probably involved the sacrifice of animals. Banned from participating in the tribe's central spiritual and social activity the punishment was severe indeed, they were outcasts, and perhaps became scapegoats too, left alone to be tortured by their own sense of shame, and the derision of the tribe. Such ostracism was a dreadful punishment, inconceivable to the modern individualist mind. Caesar explains it: 'Those that are so banned are reckoned as impious and criminal; all men move out of their path and shun their approach and conversation, for fear they may get some harm from their contact.' Ireland was never conquered by Rome, but there too we have further substantiation for the theory that ostracism was the severest punishment of the Druids when we study early Irish law, a direct descendant of Druidic law. Banishment was the heaviest of punishments – those who had committed incest or murder for example were cast into the sea in a coracle with nothing but a knife to help them fend for themselves. If they returned alive they were allowed to live – they had endured a trial by the elements and the torment of being outcast and of facing death and were considered thus purified. They must surely have known the tides well, for no-one would have wanted a murderer to be washed back to shore an hour later with a knife in his hand. Cynics would say that the buck was being passed, with each community wafting their criminals downstream to each other. Those with a knowledge of the sea and its dangers will know that many would have perished if set adrift at certain places and at certain times.

If the Druids' severest punishment was banishment or exile, either literal as in being cast into the sea or social and psychological as in being banned from worship, then why do we have the association of Druidry with human sacrifice? Let us look at Caesar's *De Bello Gallico* again:

> The whole nation of the Gauls is greatly devoted to ritual observances, and for that reason those who are smitten with the more grievous maladies and who are engaged in the perils of battle either sacrifice human victims or vow so to do, employing the Druids as ministers for such sacrifices. . . . Others use figures of immense size, whose limbs, woven out of twigs, they fill with living men and set on fire.

In both cases it is the Gauls, not the Druids who perform or vow to perform the sacrifices. In the sentence referring to the wicker figures no mention of Druids is made. In the earlier sentence it is stated that the Gauls employed the Druids as ministers for such sacrifices. Until capital punishment was abolished, the British employed Christian priests as ministers when the convicted were hanged. And still today we see the armed forces employing Christian ministers as battle is waged and thousands are sacrificed to the God of War. Professor Piggott feels that a body of men such as the Druids, with their depth of wisdom, mathematical, poetical and judicial skill, must have somehow approved of or been involved in the sacrifices: 'The Druids were the wise men of barbarian Celtic society, and Celtic religion was their religion, with all its crudities. It is sheer romanticism and a capitulation to the myth of the Noble Savage to imagine that they stood by the sacrifices in duty bound but with disapproval in their faces and elevated thoughts in their minds.'[11]

Professor Piggott would presumably allow a modern Christian priest to have feelings of concern for the victim of execution or for the souls of the soldiers or sailors under his care, but a Druid could clearly have had no such feelings. Even though he was a philosopher and sage, learned in myth and poetry, he was a barbarian – a crude primitive and must therefore have had a lust for blood. Professor Piggott tries hard to present his view of Druidry as objective and factual, and yet he is unable to free himself of his prejudices, and his book becomes subjectivity masquerading as objectivity. He knows that mankind has made extraordinary advances in scientific understanding but has failed to notice that our moral and philosophical development has made no such similar strides. Even though thousands of years old, the purity and sophistication of the ethics and philosophy of the Greeks, the Gnostics, and the Buddhists, to mention but a few traditions, testifies to the fact that at all times the sages of this world have had access to the sublime truths, and there is no reason to presume that the Druids were any different in this respect.

DRUIDS AS TEACHERS

A great number of young men gather about them for the sake of instruction and hold them in great honour. . . . Tempted by these great rewards [exemption from military service and war taxes] many young men assemble of their own motion to receive their training; many are sent by parents and relatives. Report says that in the schools of the Druids they learn by heart a great number of verses, and therefore some persons remain twenty years under training. And they do not think it proper to commit these utterances to writing, although in almost all other matters, and in their public and private accounts, they make use of Greek letters.

Caesar – *De Bello Gallico*

It is clear from both the classical and the Irish sources that one of the main functions of the Druid was as a teacher. This involved teaching at both an esoteric and an exoteric level. Caitlín Matthews offers the image of the Jewish rabbi to help us picture how a Druid might have lived and worked. She or he was: 'a man or woman of wisdom whose advice was sought on all matters of daily life, one who perhaps also fulfilled a craft, one who was married and had a family, one who brought the people together for common celebrations and whose word was law. Like the Hasidic rabbis who practised qabbala and were known as seers and wonder-workers, so too, the druid was a person of unusual skills. . . . From the various Celtic accounts, we find that a druid usually had one or more students attached to his retinue or household. Again, to return to our Jewish parallel, a rabbi would often run a talmudic school for anything from a handful to a number of students. Similarly, druidic students learned from their masters and mistresses.'[12]

While some Druids may have simply had one or two students living with them, helping, presumably, with the household routine in return for training, others gathered around them sufficient numbers of disciples to form a veritable college of Druidry. In Ulster, for example, it is recorded that Cathbad, one of King Conchobar's Druids, was surrounded by a hundred students.

What would they have learned? Just as the monastic orders later became the centres of learning, the Druid colleges, large and small, were in charge of the whole spectrum of education from the teaching of general education to that of philosophy, from the teaching of law to the teaching of magic, from the teaching of healing skills to the teaching of the correct order of ceremonial. We also know that Druids acted as tutors to the children of kings and nobles, and that students would be sent from one Druid master to another to learn different skills. One of the arguments for supporting the idea that Druidry originated in Britain with the fusion of Celtic tradition and the existing priesthood of the megalithic culture lies in the fact that students were sent from Gaul to Britain to be trained in Druidry. They were sent to the fountainhead of Druid culture – to imbibe at its source. Caesar supports this view when he says: 'It is believed that their rule of life was discovered in Britain and transferred thence to Gaul; and today those who would study the subject more accurately journey, as a rule, to Britain to learn it.'[13]

It is intriguing to think that the roots of our education system lie in Druidry, just as do the roots of our criminal investigation and judicial systems. One day we will perhaps see the statue of a Druid outside New Scotland Yard or the law courts in the Strand, or a mural in the lobby of the Department of Education depicting a Druid teaching within a grove of trees.

DRUIDS AS KINGS AND ADVISERS TO KINGS

There is evidence that some kings were also Druids. The Druid Ailill Aulomon was King of Munster in the first century AD and it is recorded that three Druid kings ruled in 'the Isle of Thule'.[14] Thule was the name often given to Iceland, and here lies the fascinating possibility that Iceland was a kingdom once ruled by Druids, long before its Viking conquest. The official history of Iceland states that the first Norse colonisers, arriving in AD 874 found and drove away a few isolated Irish hermits, who had journeyed there via the Faroe Islands. But recent work on Icelandic blood-group types shows them to have a greater similarity to those of Ireland than of Scandinavia. This leads one to agree with those historians who claim that Iceland had in fact been colonised by the Celts long before the Vikings arrived. This claim gains further support when we learn that the only extant manuscript source of information that we have about the Nordic pagan cosmology, the Edda, was written in Iceland and not in Scandinavia. The manuscript looks remarkably like the early Irish manuscripts of the same period, and it is tempting to see the Vikings of Iceland being helped to record their cosmology by Irish Druids, or their descendants.

To return to Britain and Ireland, when Druids were not kings, they were advisers to kings, and were accorded such status that they were often the first to speak at official functions. At the court of Conchobar, King of Ulster, for example, no one had the right to speak before the Druid had spoken.

DRUIDS AS SCIENTISTS AND INVENTORS

We know that the Druids concerned themselves with what we today term the sciences. To what degree their mathematics was numerology, their chemistry alchemy, their astronomy astrology, we will never know. But we do know that the building of the stone circles required sophisticated measuring, calculating and engineering skills, and that this same building depended upon a knowledge of the movement of the heavens to such a degree that they were clearly skilled astronomers.

The work of Sir Norman Lockyer, Professors Hawkins, Atkinson, and Thom, and John Michell amongst others, shows us that these men were scientists indeed, creating giant astronomical computers in stone. Some writers have even suggested that the Druids might have invented the telescope, basing this idea on the statement of Diodorus Siculus, who said that in an island west of Celtae the Druids brought the sun and moon near to them, and on the statement of Hecataeus, who tells us that the Druids taught of the existence of lunar mountains. Others have suggested that they discovered gunpowder, but like the Chinese, used it for special effects rather than warfare. John Smith in his *Galic Antiquities* of 1780 wrote:

> Among the arcana of nature which our Druids were acquainted with, there are many presumptive, if not positive, proofs for placing the art of gunpowder, or artificial thunder and lightning; though like all other mysteries, they kept the invention of it a secret.

We have no hard historical evidence for this suggestion, but it is delightful to think that the Druid would amaze and entertain his entourage with fireworks, as does the Druidic figure of Gandalf in Tolkien's *Lord of the Rings*.

While they may or may not have experimented with fireworks, they certainly worked with fire and with metals. Their esoteric work with fire is a matter of inner knowledge, for it deals with their ability to relate to and work with the sacred fire within the body as well as within the grove. Their work with metal might well have been alchemical. There is certainly a strong element of alchemy in later Druidry. Since fire, like water, was and is considered sacred by all those with a spiritual understanding of the natural world, we can be sure that the Druids were masters of fire. Metal-working in early societies was also considered a sacred art, for upon it depended the tribe's ability to defend itself and to gain food from the earth or from animals. The Welsh tradition states that a branch of Druids, known as the Pheryllt, worked as metallurgists and alchemists in the magical city of Emrys in Snowdonia. This 'ambrosial city' was also known as Dinas Affaraon, the 'city of the higher powers'.

The Druid as metal-worker would have forged the swords for kings and nobles which would have been imbued during their casting and annealing with magical spells designed to protect the bearer and ensure him victory. The sword figures largely in the Druid mythos: It emerges out of the two fixed elements of water and earth in the Arthurian legend: being pulled out of stone by Arthur, and being raised mysteriously out of the Lake when needed. It is born in fire with the skill of the Druid-Alchemist, and it is raised in the air during the Order's Beltane ceremony, as the sword-bearer cries: 'Behold this sword Excalibur, which rose from the lake of still meditation and was returned to it again. The sword of spirit, of light and truth, is always sharp and always with us, if our lake be stilled.'[15] At a spiritual-psychological level, the sword represents the Will. When the Will is not aligned to our higher values and purpose it runs amok, and the sword becomes the weapon which maims and destroys. When it is aligned with higher purpose it becomes the sword of spirit, a representation of our ability to be spiritual warriors in a world filled with difficulties which require the warrior spirit to overcome them. In the Druid circle the sword is placed in the South, just as the wand is placed in the East, the cup of water in the West, and the stone in the North. We can surmise too that the Druids as metalworkers would have cast the sacred cauldrons. Just as the sword represents the 'male' directive qualities of mind and spirit, so does the cauldron represent the 'female' inclusive qualities of heart and soul. And just as the sword figures largely in Druid ceremonial and mythology, so too does the cauldron, representing, at its roots, the origin of the grail symbol.

DRUIDS AS PHILOSOPHERS

> Some say that the study of philosophy was of barbarian origin. For the Persians had their Magi, the Babylonians or the Assyrians the Chaldeans, the Indians their Gymnosophists, while the Kelts and the Galatae had seers called Druids and Semnotheoi.
>
> Diogenes Laertius – *Lives of the Philosophers* circa AD 250

In examining the roles of the Druid as teacher and judge, king and adviser to kings, scientist and inventor, we must remember that behind each of these functions the Druid was at heart a philosopher. His or her concern was with the meaning and purpose of life on earth, and it was for this reason that Strabo wrote '. . . the Druids, in addition to natural philosophy, study also moral philosophy'.

To divide their roles in the way we have done here, is for the sake of convenience only, for in reality the roles merged and combined, as we can see when Caesar tells us 'They have many discussions as touching the stars and their movement, the size of the universe and of the earth, the order of nature, the strength and the powers of the immortal gods, and hand down their lore to the young men.'[16] Here we see them as scientists, as astronomers and mathematicians, as philosophers discussing the powers of the gods, and as teachers passing on their wisdom.

In contemporary Druidry, the tree which represents the Druid Grade is the Oak, the regal tree of wisdom and tradition, the primordial tree that has always been associated with both Druids and their *Nemeton*, the oak groves where they gathered and taught. The East is the place of the Druid, for it is from the East that the sun rises and from which illumination comes. The times associated with the Druid Grade are noon and Summer – times of greatest brightness and growth.

The Bard in his training has opened to the artist that lives within him, the Ovate in his training has opened to the shaman who lives within – to the one who can travel in the inner realms to explore the elastic nature of time, and the inner power of trees, herbs and animals. The Druid, in his training, opens to the Druid within. A circular statement perhaps, but one which is fully understandable to the Druid himself.

At present, the only Druid group in Britain that gives training at all three levels is the Order of Bards, Ovates and Druids. It is helpful, when we consider the three stages or groupings, if we do not consider them as a hierarchy, a ladder we must climb in order to reach enlightenment or full empowerment, but rather as levels of deepening. There is a path, or journey, that can be taken from one grade to the next, but having reached the Druid Grade the journey can begin again, making it one that follows a spiral or circular path rather than a linear one. At the Druid level the injunction is given: Generate and Regenerate! To do this we must die, we must change. The Ovate experience is passed through, under the sign of the Yew: we follow the injunction 'Die and be reborn!' Finally we reach the stage of the Bard and we are able to be creative, to be fully born in the world, to express our inherent divinity in word, song, art and music.

The three realms of Art, Nature and Philosophy are encompassed within the three divisions of the Druid Tradition. We are finally able to unite our artistic concerns with our environmental and spiritual concerns. The Bard, Ovate and Druid are one person standing on the earth – poet and shaman, healer and philosopher – spiritual and earthy.

We ourselves may well not be this 'Whole Person', able to encompass all these abilities and interests, but the Druid as a model is always there [and has always been there for thousands of years] to encourage and guide us, to shine a light for us on a path that is not uniform and not pre-determined, but unique to us and built with our own experience and our own creative genius. According to your belief and experience you will understand this image as a metaphor, as a cultural creation, as an archetype in the collective consciousness, or as an actual being or host of beings who exist on the inner planes and who are simply waiting for us to turn to them for guidance.

EXERCISE – 4

Having read this chapter, choose a piece of music that you find particularly effective in inspiring you and helping you to 'change gear' – to change consciousness. Spend a few moments forgetting all that you have read, making yourself comfortable, and allowing yourself to come to a sense of inner centredness and calm. Listen to the music, and as you do so, let all disturbing thoughts be laid aside. Close your eyes, and focus for a few moments on your breathing as you allow the music to flow through you. If you wish, feel yourself bathed in the light and warmth of the sun, or imagine that you are lying on the ground, looking up at a myriad of stars in the night sky.

When the music finishes, allow yourself to stay as long as you wish in the state of consciousness that the music has taken you to. At some point, drop into your consciousness this seed-question, 'How can I awaken the Creative Self within me?' Understand this term in its widest sense, as representing that inner potential that we all have to be creative in our lives.

An answer to this question may rise up in your awareness, or it may not. An unanswered question that we drop into the still pool of our awareness can be evocative and effective in a way that becomes clear only at a later date. When you feel ready, become aware of being fully present in your physical body – here and now. Open your eyes, and stretch before standing up or continuing with the next chapter.

5 · THE EIGHTFOLD YEAR
THE DRUID CEREMONIES
AND THEIR MEANINGS

Mankind has got to get back to the rhythm of the Cosmos.
D. H. Lawrence

Since the Enlightenment our culture has projected the message that life is linear – that we are born, we grow old and we die, and that's it. The old message of the cyclicity of life, of life as a circle or spiral, that humanity intuitively knew from the dawn of time, and whose symbols were carved on stones all over the world, was replaced a few hundred years ago by the symbol of the straight line: the male, linear, scientific world-view that, in distortion, worships progress and goal-achievement above wisdom and clarity of being.

One of the results of this change in the collective consciousness from an awareness of the circularity of life to its linearity, has been a disconnection in the souls of many people from one of the most nourishing of spiritual sources, the realm of nature.

When I met the old Chief Druid, Nuinn, he spoke of a way that had never severed its connection with nature, and which conveyed a sense of the immanence of the divine in all things. In Druidry you communed with God in the 'temple not made with hands', in the 'eye of the sun', in the open air, in the environment made by God not by humans. In Druidry God was seen as being in everything, omnipresent yet manifesting differently in stone and star, tree and celandine.

I was introduced to a way of orienting my life that meant I could be in tune with nature, not separate from it. Looking back, I now realise what an extraordinary gift it was for me to have been given such a way of understanding life at such an early age. My teacher explained the festival scheme, the central observance-pattern of Druidry, to me one day in this way:

'Take your life and its events. Place them in one line with birth at one end and death at the other end', he said to me in a café, picking up a knife to illustrate his point, 'and you have an isolated line beginning in the void and terminating in the void. Other lines might run parallel to yours, collide or cross, but they will all end as they begun – with nothing.' He paused, looked at me with a shrug, and then said 'But we know life isn't really like that. We know that death is followed by rebirth because we see it with the rebirth of life in the Spring, and, if we are lucky, we remember it when we reach far back in our own memories. So life is like this,' he said gesturing to the plate, 'Not this!' [putting the knife down with a touch of theatre, as people started to look at us in the café.]

He then ran his finger around the circumference of the plate, saying, 'You are born, you grow old, you die' bringing his finger back to the starting point, and then again 'You are born, you are a child, a young man, an old man, you die. You are born, you die,' and so on, several times until he put the plate down to allow the waitress to serve our meal.

'What is it that guides the course of this cycle – this circling?' He asked me. My mind went blank for a moment. 'What lies at the centre of this wheel? What or who is responsible for its turning?' I got it: 'My soul – my true identity that endures through every life!' 'Exactly,' he said, placing a pat of butter in the centre of my dish of spaghetti to mark the place of my Soul.

'Now let us forget the individual,' he went on, 'and look at the world. The seasons are clearly cyclical – one following the other inexorably. So we can place them on a circle. That is the circle of the year. But the life of each day we can place on a circle too – it is born at dawn, reaches its peak at noon, and passes from dusk into night, before being reborn again the next day.' He began circling his plate with his finger, more gingerly now, to avoid the food.

'The circle of the year and the circle of the day have affinities. Winter is like the dead of night, when all is still. Spring is like the dawn of the day when the birds awaken and praise the sun. Summer is like noon – a time of maximum heat and growth. Autumn is like the evening, when the autumn colours seem like the colours of the sunset. So there are the two cycles of the Earth harmoniously brought together. Who or what do you think it is that controls the turning of this wheel?' he said, taking the opportunity finally to begin eating, and also taking great pleasure in the coincidence that now he needed to turn his spaghetti on a fork, which operation he naturally chose to perform in the centre of the plate. Again, for a moment my mind went blank. 'God?' I said. 'Well, yes, God is at the centre and is the cause of everything. But what specifically causes the cycle of the day and the seasons on Earth is the Sun. The Sun causes the wheel to turn.'

I thought about this and realised it was true. Leaning forward he peered at me intently for a moment, before asking his next question: 'And what do you think the connection is between your cycle' he said, pointing to my plate, 'and the cycle of the earth?' pointing to his plate. For the moment I could see no connection – they seemed entirely separate as were our two plates of spaghetti. Nuinn circled his plate with his finger once more. 'Birth, death, rebirth. Winter Solstice – the longest night. Will the sun be reborn? Yes! And here, opposite, at the Summer Solstice he is at his maximum strength, at the time of the longest day.' Pointing to the top of my plate, he said 'Here you are born, incarnated as a spark of light, and there,' pointing to the other side of my plate, 'you are in the prime of your life.' He suddenly grabbed the pepper pot and made a dash of pepper on my plate at these two points, saying 'Summer, Winter.' And then two further splashes were made to either side: 'Spring and Autumn.' Pointing at each mark, he continued 'Here we see how the cycle of your life and the life of the Earth are entwined. The Spring is the time of your childhood, the Summer the time of your manhood, the Autumn the time of your maturity in old age, and Winter is the time of your death. At the centre of the turning wheel of your life is your Soul. At the centre of the turning wheel of the Earth is the Sun.' He looked around the table for something to use, then with a flourish he tossed a spoonful of parmesan cheese into the centre of my half-eaten pile of spaghetti. 'The Sun and your Soul! Now perhaps you know why the Sun is revered so much in Druidry.'

At this point I experienced one of those sudden rushes of insight in which everything seems to come together and make sense in one flash, even though one's everyday mind cannot quite grasp all the connections. 'This is perhaps why it is said that the Druids believed that our Souls originate in the Sun. They believed that between lives we go to rest on the moon until our last three incarnations on earth, when we are allowed to rest between lives in the heart of the Sun, with those golden Solar Beings who guide the destiny of our planet.'

THE EIGHTFOLD SCHEME

That was my introduction to the Eightfold Scheme that lies at the heart of Druidry, and indeed the Western Pagan Tradition, of which Druidry is one manifestation and Wicca another. Both Druids and Witches celebrate these eight festivals, although in a different way, and with different rites.

Basing itself on this deep and mysterious connection between the source of our individual lives and the source of the life of the planet, Druidry recognises eight particular times during the yearly cycle which are significant and which are marked by special observances.

Of the eight times, four are solar and four are lunar, creating thereby a balanced scheme of interlocking masculine and feminine observances. The solar observances are the ones that most people associate with modern-day Druids, particularly the Summer Solstice ceremonies at Stonehenge. At the Solstices, the Sun is revered at the point of its apparent death at midwinter and of its maximum power at the noon of the year when the days are longest. At the Equinoxes, day and night are balanced. At the Spring Equinox on 21 March, the power of the sun is on the increase, and we celebrate the time of sowing and of preparation for the gifts of Summer. At the Autumnal Equinox on 21 September, although day and night are of equal duration, the power of the sun is on the wane, and we give thanks for the gifts of the harvest and prepare for the darkness of Winter. These four festivals are astronomical observances, and we can be sure our ancestors marked them with ritual because many of the stone circles are oriented to their points of sunrise or sunset. By the time the circles were built, our ancestors had become a pastoral people, and times of sowing and reaping were vital to them.

But as well as these four astronomical, solar festivals, there exist four times in the year which were and are also considered sacred. These were the times which were more associated with the livestock cycle, rather than the farming cycle. At Samhuinn, between 31 October and 2 November, livestock for whom there was insufficient fodder were slaughtered and their meat salted and stored. At Imbolc, on 2 February the lambs were born. At Beltane, on 1 May, it was the time of mating and of the passing of the livestock through the two Beltane fires for purification. Lughnasadh, on 1 August, was the time which marked the link between the agricultural and the livestock cycle – the harvest began and both human food and animal fodder were reaped and stored.

The two sets of festivals represent far more than just times which our ancestors chose to honour the plant and animal life-cycles though. They demonstrate our thorough interconnectedness with both the animal and plant realms. It is only we moderns who can separate the life-cycles in an analytical way.

As we contemplate the festivals we shall see how interwoven is the life of our psyche and of our body, of the planet and of the sun and moon, for each festival time marks a potent conjunction of Time and Place in a way that is quite remarkable. Looking at the complete cycle, we shall begin at Samhuinn – a time which marked traditionally the ending and the beginning of the Celtic Year.

Samhuinn, from 31 October to 2 November was a time of no-time. Celtic society, like all early societies, was highly structured and organised, everyone knew their place. But to allow that order to be psychologically comfortable, the Celts knew that there had to be a time when order and structure were abolished, when chaos could reign. And Samhuinn was such a time. Time was abolished for the three days of this festival and people did crazy things, men dressed as women and women as men. Farmers' gates were unhinged and left in ditches, peoples' horses were moved to different fields, and children would knock on neighbours' doors for food and treats in a way that we still find today, in a watered-down way, in the custom of trick-or-treating on Hallowe'en.

But behind this apparent lunacy, lay a deeper meaning. The Druids knew that these three days had a special quality about them. The veil between this world and the World of the Ancestors was drawn aside on these nights, and for those who were prepared, journeys could be made in safety to the 'other side'. The Druid rites, therefore, were concerned with making contact with the spirits of the departed, who were seen as sources of guidance and inspiration rather than as sources of dread. The dark moon, the time when no moon can be seen in the sky, was the phase of the moon which ruled this time, because it represents a time in which our mortal sight needs to be obscured in order for us to see into the other worlds.

The dead are honoured and feasted, not as the dead, but as the living spirits of loved ones and of guardians who hold the root-wisdom of the tribe. With the coming of Christianity, this festival was turned into Hallowe'en [October 31] All Hallows [1 November] and All Saints [2 November]. Here we can see most clearly the way in which Christianity built on the pagan foundations it found rooted in these isles. Not only does the purpose of the festival match with the earlier one, but even the unusual length of the festival is the same.

Next in the cycle is the time of the Winter Solstice, called in the Druid Tradition Alban Arthuan [the Light of Arthur]. This is the time of death and rebirth. The sun appears to be abandoning us completely as the longest night comes to us. Linking our own inner journey to the yearly cycle, the words of the Druid ceremony urge us to 'Cast away, O wo/man whatever impedes the appearance of light.' In darkness we throw on to the ground the scraps of material we have been carrying that signify those things which have been holding us back, and one lamp is lit from a flint and raised up on the Druid's crook in the East. The year is reborn and a new cycle begins, which will reach its peak at the time of the Midsummer Solstice, before returning again to the place of death-and-birth.

Although the Bible indicates that Jesus was born in the Spring, it is no accident that the early Church chose to move his official birthday to the time of the Midwinter Solstice, for it is indeed when the Light enters the darkness of the World, and we see again the building of Christianity on the foundations of earlier belief.

In a Christian culture we really only have one marker for the year, and that is Christmas. Easter and Harvest-time used to be significant, but can hardly be considered so now, when only a fraction of the British population attend Church regularly. Druidry has eight markers, which means that every six weeks or so, we have the opportunity to step out of the humdrum of daily life, to honour the conjunction of Place and Time.

The next Festival occurs on 2 February, or the night of 1 February. It is called Imbolc in the Druid tradition, or sometimes Oimelc. Although we would think of Imbolc as being in the midst of Winter, it represents in fact the first of a trio of Spring celebrations, since it is the time of the first appearance of the snowdrop, and of the melting of the snows and the clearing of the debris of Winter. It is a time when we sense the first glimmer of Spring, and when lambs are born. In the Druid tradition it is a gentle, beautiful festival in which the Mother Goddess is honoured with eight candles rising out of the water at the centre of the ceremonial circle.

The Goddess that ruled Samhuinn was the Cailleach, the Grey Hag, the Mountain Mother, the Dark Woman of Knowledge. But by Imbolc the Goddess has become Brighid, the Goddess of poets, healers and midwives. And so we often use Imbolc as a time for an Eisteddfod dedicated to poetry and song praising the Goddess in her many forms. The Christian development of this festival is Candlemas – the time of

71

the Presentation of Christ in the Temple. For years successive Popes had tried to stop parades of lit candles in the streets of Rome at this time, until seeing that it was impossible to put a stop to this pagan custom, it was suggested that the populace enter the churches so that the priests could bless the candles.

Time moves on, and in a short while we come to the Spring Equinox, the time of equality of day and night, when the forces of light are on the increase. At the centre of the trio of Spring Festas, Alban Eiler [the Light of the Earth] marks the more recognisable beginnings of Spring, when the flowers are beginning to appear and when the sowing begins in earnest. As the point of psychological development in our lives it marks the time of late childhood to, say, 14 years – Imbolc marking the time of early childhood [say to 7 years]. We are in the Spring of our lives – the seeds that are planted in our childhood time of Imbolc and Alban Eiler will flower from the Beltane time of adolescence onwards as capacities and powers that will help us to negotiate our lives with skill and accomplishment.

Beltane, on 1 May marks the time of our adolescence and early wo/manhood. Spring is in full bloom, and twin fires would be lit at this time, through which would be passed the cattle after their long winter confinement, or over which those hoping for a child or good fortune would leap. When I was young, the Order celebrated Beltane on Glastonbury Tor. The celebration of the union of male and female is symbolically depicted there in the landscape, with Chalice Well representing the feminine and the Tor representing the masculine principle. We see traces of the Beltane celebrations on May Day, when dancing round the maypole celebrates the fertility of the land and creates an echo of the ritual circle dances that must have been enacted in stone circles throughout the country.

We have reached the time of the Summer Solstice, Alban Heruin, The Light of the Shore, by 21 or 22 June [the dates for each of the solar festivals vary each year since the events are astronomical not man-made, like our calendar]. Light is at its maximum, and this is the time of the longest day. It is at this time that the Druids hold their most complex ceremony. Starting at midnight on the eve of the Solstice, a vigil is held through the night, seated around the Solstice fire. The night is over in a matter of hours, and as light breaks, the Dawn Ceremony marks the time of the sun's rising on this his most powerful day. At noon a further ceremony is held. It is the dawn ceremony at Stonehenge which has attracted so much publicity, and which has been banned for the past two years, amidst much public outcry. Six weeks later we come to the time of Lughnasadh on 1

August, which marks the beginning of harvest time. The hay would have been gathered in, and the time for reaping the wheat and barley was due. It was a time of gathering together, of contests and games and of marriages. The marriages contracted at this time could be annulled at the same time the following year, offering the couple a sensible 'trial period'. In some areas a flaming wheel was sent rolling down the hillside at this time to symbolise the descent of the year towards Winter, and in the Druid ceremony a wheel is passed around the circle in symbol of the turning year. The Christian version of this festival is Lammas, which has recently been revived in some churches. The word Lammas comes from *hlafmasse* – 'loaf-mass' – since bread is offered at this time from the newly harvested grain.

The Autumnal Equinox, on 21 September or thereabouts, is called Alban Elued or Light of the Water in the Druid tradition. It represents the second of the harvest festivals, this time marking the end of harvest-time, just as Lughnasadh marked its beginning. Again day and night are equally balanced as they were at the time of the Spring Equinox, but soon the nights will grow longer than the days and Winter will be with us. In the ceremony we give thanks for the fruits of the earth and for the goodness of the Mother Goddess. And so the circle completes itself as we come again to the time of Samhuinn – the time of death and of rebirth. (See figure 3 on p. 74).

THE RELEVANCE AND VALUE OF THE FESTIVALS

What does it mean to celebrate these festivals? Are we simply trying to revive customs that belong to a different era, and are well forgotten? Those who follow Druidry believe strongly that this is not the case. Just as Christmas and New Year are vital to our psychic health because they give us some measure of the passage of our lives, so does the recognition and celebration of the eight festival times enable us to attune our personal rhythm to the rhythm of the cosmos, of nature. By doing this we find that we develop an increasing sense of peace and place in our world and in our lives.

Let us look at the value of the festivals from a psychological point of view. When we celebrate them we honour times which have been considered sacred for over four thousand years. We know this because the stone circles were orientated to their sunrise points [see Chapter 7]. The four fire festivals relate to key life periods and the experiences necessary for each one of them: Imbolc invokes the purity and mothering that we need in our first years on earth. We need the stillness of Imbolc, of the candles glittering on the water, of

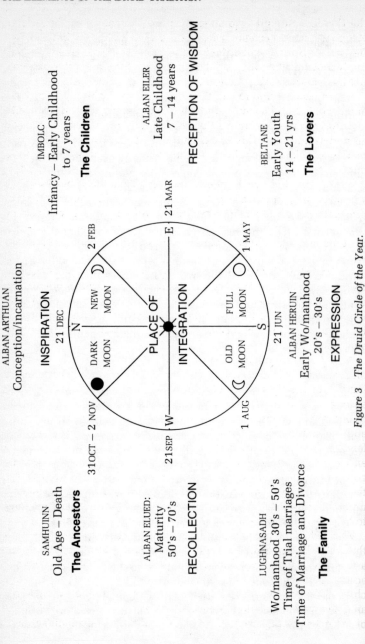

Figure 3   The Druid Circle of the Year.

IMBOLC
Infancy – Early Childhood
to 7 years
The Children

ALBAN EILER
Late Childhood
7 – 14 years
RECEPTION OF WISDOM

BELTANE
Early Youth
14 – 21 yrs
The Lovers

ALBAN ARTHUAN
Conception/incarnation
INSPIRATION
21 DEC

ALBAN HERUIN
Early Wo/manhood
20's – 30's
EXPRESSION

SAMHUINN
Old Age – Death
The Ancestors

ALBAN ELUED:
Maturity
50's – 70's
RECOLLECTION

LUGHNASADH
Wo/manhood 30's – 50's
Time of Trial marriages
Time of Marriage and Divorce
The Family

INTEGRATION

PLACE OF INTEGRATION

NEW MOON
DARK MOON
FULL MOON
OLD MOON

N
E
S
W

2 FEB
21 MAR
1 MAY
21 JUN
1 AUG
21 SEP
31 OCT – 2 NOV

the Goddess Brighid who sings to us each night as we fall asleep. When we have become young adults, we need the initiation of Beltane, of Spring, when the force of our sexuality courses through our blood and when we need the guidance of the tribe and its mythos, not its denial or salaciousness.

As we become young adults at the Lughnasadh time of our lives and begin to build a family, the rules change – the wildness of youth gives way to the constraints that responsibility brings, and we need an understanding of this as part of the wider scheme of things – not merely as a 'knuckling down' to duty with the seeds of rebellion in our hearts.

As we grow old, we approach the Gateway to the Other World. If we have followed such a path as Druidry, this becomes a time of preparation for the Great Adventure, a time in which we become familiar with our friends and guides in the Other Worlds who show us, time and again, that death is really a birth to another level – a wider horizon.

If we work with this scheme, we have a chance to invoke each of these phases of our life every year, as if each year were a microcosm of our complete lives. In the early Spring we open to the child who lives in each one of us – we honour and acknowledge and cherish him, and we allow the healing breath of the Goddess of Poetry to sing gently to him.

At Beltane, we open to the God and Goddess of Youth. However old we are, Spring makes us feel young again, and at Beltane we jump over the fires of vitality and youth and allow that vitality to enliven and heal us. When young we might use this time as an opportunity to connect to our sensuality in a positive creative way, and when older the mating that we seek might well be one of the feminine and masculine sides of our nature. Integration of the male and female aspects of the Self has long been seen as one of the prime goals of spiritual and psychotherapeutic work, and Beltane represents the time when we can open to this work fully, allowing the natural union of polarities that occurs in nature at this time the opportunity to help us in our work – a work that is essentially alchemical.

We move from conjunction to the fruits of that conjunction with the festival time of Lughnasadh – the harvest being that of either a family or of creative works. This is a time of satisfaction in our accomplishments, whether that means gazing into the face of our child or feeling the warm satisfaction that comes when we achieve an objective in our field of endeavour. It is at the time of the festival of Lughnasadh that we can invoke the powers of accomplishment to nourish the need that we all have to achieve something in this world. If we feel that we have achieved something, we can use this time to open ourselves to the satisfaction this brings. So often we rush through life that we do not even pause to enjoy those things which we have around us, such as our family or home. If we feel that we have not yet achieved anything, now is the time to open ourselves to our potential for achievement. Acting 'as if' is a powerful way to mould our future. If we spend time opening ourselves to the feeling of family or accomplishment, even though we do not apparently have these things, we help to invoke these realities for the future.

Finally, at the time of Samhuinn we can open ourselves to the reality of other worlds, to the reality of the existence of those of our friends who have 'gone before us' and who are still alive and well, though not on this earth. If each year we have in consciousness connected to this plane, when the time comes for our transfer, it will represent a more familiar, if still challenging territory that we will actively want to explore. Children brought up in this tradition will have a warm feeling towards this other realm, rather than being filled with fear of the Unknown, or with a fear that has been provoked by the pernicious images of hell developed by distorted forms of Christianity.

We have seen how the four fire festivals demonstrate a cycle related to the phases of our life on earth. The four solar festivals represent, at a psychological level, four key functions or processes: Inspiration, Reception, Expression, and Recollection. The Winter Solstice, Alban Arthuan, represents a time when we can open to the forces of Inspiration and Conception. All about us is darkness. Our only guide is Arthur, the Great Bear, the Pole Star. In the stillness of night is Intuition born. Both the festival and the function is located in the north, realm of the night and mid-winter. The Winter Solstice is the time when the atom-seed of Light, represented both by the one light raised on high and by the white mistletoe berries distributed during the ceremony, comes down from the inspired realms and is conceived or incarnated in the womb of the night and of the Earth Mother. It is thus a potent time to open ourselves to the fertilising power of the Muse or of the Great Source.

The Spring Equinox, Alban Eiler, located in the east, represents the time of Reception – Reception of Wisdom, as we face the dawn rays of the rising sun on the first morning of Spring. The east has always been associated with Wisdom and Enlightenment, because it is from the east that the sun rises. And it is on the Spring Equinox that it rises due east. At this time we can open ourselves to wisdom and the powers that can bring clarity to us.

The Summer Solstice, Alban Heruin, in the south, is the time of Expression, when we can open ourselves to realising our dreams and working in the arena of the outer world. The Summer always seems the time when there is the most energy for getting things done, and aware of this, we can cooperate with this energy. We often take holidays at this time, and while it is a good time for active holidays, the restful, tranquil break from the hurly burly of life is probably best taken in the Autumn, around the time of Alban Elued, located in the west, when the energy moves towards one that fosters Recollection – the quiet in-gathering of the experience of Summer.

Working every six weeks or so with a psychological process or function or with a life-period is a deeply satisfying experience.

The lines of connection between the festivals on opposite sides of the circle are also worth exploring.

The dynamic that runs from north to south, operating between the two Solstices, is one of incarnation, manifestation, creation. The inspiration and realisation of Midwinter is grounded and given birth in the realm of matter and expression at the time of the Summer Solstice.

The dynamic that runs from east to west, operating between the two Equinoxes, is one of elaboration and construction. The wisdom and clarity received in the Spring is elaborated and developed by the psyche and is built into its very fabric through the process of rumination and contemplation that occurs in the Autumn, at the time of the setting sun.

The dynamic that runs from Beltane in the south-east, to Samhuinn in the north-west, is one of Karma – by mating we create the cycle of birth and death, and we thereby invoke the operation of Karma. The joy of sexuality and union is counterbalanced by our fear of death and separation, but both are part of the same dynamic which represents the dance of Creation. Both festivals mark processes which represent Great Adventures – our sexual world is full of mystery and the Unknown, of love and the exploration of the depths of feelings, just as is the world of death. Both somehow also represent Independence, for we enter our first sexual experiences with an intense feeling of our individuality and uniqueness just as we enter the Gateway of death supremely alone. The adolescent who leaves home is under the sign of Beltane and is working with the Spirit of Independence, just as the dying too are struggling to feel comfortable with being on their own when facing the Great Adventure.

The dynamic that runs from Imbolc in the north-east to Lughnasadh in the south-west is one that is also linked to Karma, although here it is a dynamic of Dependence, rather than Independence, for it represents the relationship between Infancy, at the time of Imbolc and the Family, at the time of Lughnasadh. Both are times when we are dependent on others, and when we need to attune to the dynamic of dependence rather than independence. Our adolescents and the elderly need help to come to terms with what it means to be a separate individual. Our children and parents need help to come to terms with the strain that having to be dependent on others can bring.

At the centre of the circle – the point at which all these pathways meet – is the place of Integration. Here all the qualities and dynamics find their resting place and place of creative union at the very heart of the circle, which is also at the very heart of our beings. In many of the ceremonies this reality is enacted ritually by the Druid moving sacred objects from the periphery of the circle to the centre, thus enacting the movement of integration on the physical level and grounding a spiritual and psychological principle in action with his body.

The centre of the circle represents the God/dess and the Self; the Sun and our Soul; the Source of All Being. As such it is the place where all comes to rest and to fruition.

We can now see how, over the years as one practises Druidry, the circle becomes a magical place in which the circumference represents the round of our daily, yearly and whole-life journeys – inextricably tied to the daily and yearly cycle of the earth, and the eight compass directions with their associated meanings and spiritual and psychological associations. At the centre lies the still point of Being and No-Thing. The entire space of the circle becomes our sphere of inner working – it becomes a sacred area in which, like a magic carpet, we can travel to other states of being. It becomes a doorway which, like the well-known gateway of the trilithon, or henge, can give us access to previously hidden realms and altered states of consciousness. But it can only become such a vehicle with preparation and training undertaken over a considerable period of time and with much dedication.

EXERCISE – 5

Having read this chapter, spend a few moments forgetting all that you have read, make yourself comfortable, and allow yourself to come to a sense of inner centredness and calm.

Think about the time of year you find yourself in. Whatever the date is, one or other of the eight festivals will be, at the most, either three or four weeks behind or ahead of you. In other words, if it is 23 February today, Imbolc would have been celebrated three weeks ago on 2 February and the Spring Equinox is due in four weeks time on 21 or 22 March. Focus on one of these times, either behind or ahead of you. Recall the associations that this time evokes, both personal and planetary and those mentioned in the chapter you have just read. Allow your mind to explore these as much as it wishes.

Now remember the same time last year. What were you doing then? Where were you? What was your prevailing mood around that time? Can you see any connection with these things and the particular time of year? See if you can trace the journey of your life and of the world over that period. What has happened during that year? What have you learned? What have you experienced? When you feel ready, finish your period of contemplation by connecting again to a sense of peace, centredness and calm, before standing up and stretching.

6 · SPIRITS OF THE CIRCLE

From the trees Teut draws out many beautiful spirits with healing, cathartic and defensive powers, whose chief is Esus. Into the stones Teut writes the records and infuses the messages of the higher worlds.
Nuinn *The Book of Druidry*

We have seen how the circle acts as the central Druid symbol, embodying an understanding of the life of man and the life of nature and the relationship between them. We have seen how this understanding translates into a spiritual practice which honours the seasons as it honours our periods of growth and change. Soon we will learn how this symbol was manifested concretely with the building of the stone circles, but first we must come to an understanding of the spirits who were drawn to these circles and with whom the Druids worked to such effect. There is no space here to consider the spirits of the animals and the elements, of well and stream, of mountain and forest that the Druids also revered, or indeed the gods and goddesses that they worshipped, although to illustrate the richness of the tradition, we can briefly look at the god and spirit mentioned in the quotation above.

Teut, or Teutates, was the name of one of the gods, and Esus the name of one of the spirits that they revered. Trees were seen as the supreme symbol of giving – since it is they who give us food to eat, air to breathe, and the wood to house, furnish and warm us. The Druids revered the spirit of sacrifice manifested by the tree, calling it Esus or Hu-Hésus. In an extraordinary 'coincidence' of nomenclature, the Druids were using a name which hundreds of years later would be repeated to them in almost identical form. When they were told that a man called Jesus had been crucified on two planks of a tree, in a supreme act of sacrifice, it is small wonder that they reputedly replied 'Yes, we know about that.'

Rather than considering individual spirits of nature or gods in detail, let us consider those spirits which have a direct bearing on who we are, and how we guide our journey through life. We will look first at the Spirit of the Ancestors.

We know that ancestor-worship was a key component of Druidic practice. We can be sure of this because of the archaeological evidence of the megalithic culture – which in this book we see as lying at the foundations of Druidry. Anthropological studies also show us that reverence for the ancestors is a key component in nearly all religious and shamanic practices.

Today we do not worship our ancestors. We may well be interested in our family tree and in the outer achievements of our ancestors, individual or national, but we have no way of, or apparent interest in, connecting with who they were at the level of 'soul-essence'. Here we find the key to a way that modern Druidry can work with the practices of ancient Druidry in a way that is totally relevant to our times. The Druids knew that by consciously connecting with the World of the Ancestors, they could draw on a wealth of accumulated wisdom and experience that grew rather than diminished with the passing of each generation. They saw the World of the Ancestors not as some shady half-world of the dead, but as a radiant realm which represented a treasure-house of wisdom that could be accessed if one was able to travel there, or one was able to receive visitations from that realm. For that reason, the burial mounds – the chambered cairns, the round and long barrows, were built near to the sacred circles of worship. We know from archaeological evidence, that many of the cairns were kept open so that either the shaman-priests or perhaps the relatives were able to visit the burial site and commune with their departed ones. Bones have been found pointing in symbolic ways, showing that they were used for ritual purposes, as indeed bones have been for thousands of years by cultures throughout the world.

How can this be of value to us today? Although lip-service is paid to history and tradition, there is in many people a conscious or semi-conscious belief that once you're dead, you are truly 'gone', 'dead and buried', somehow no longer existent. This belief has a peculiar relevance to the environmental crisis we face. We used to believe that once we had buried something it disappeared and somehow ceased to exist. Now we discover that we can't get rid of anything! Waste tips by housing estates leak hazardous methane gas, nuclear tips leak radiation, and the sea harbours vast floating areas of dumped plastic. In a completely different way the same holds true for the dead, and although the body decays or is burned, we don't get rid of them! They continue to exist at another level and are often keen to counsel and protect us.

Druidry does not advocate spiritualism in the sense of communicating with the dead through trance-mediums, but it does teach us that we can look upon our ancestors, not as dead-and-gone, but as a rich resource that can provide us with a sense of connection to the world and to the life of humanity. When each generation stands on its own, and doesn't feel connected to its lineage, then we have the problems of alienation and disconnection which are so prevalent today. When we know about our ancestors, when we sense them as living and as supporting us, then we feel connected to the genetic life-stream, and we draw strength and nourishment from this.

In the sacred circle, the place of the Ancestors lies in the north-west – the place of the setting of the mid-Summer sun and the place of Samhuinn – when we celebrate our connection with this ancestral realm. The Spirit of the Ancestors is one which connects us to who we are as genetic beings, and we sense ourselves and our generation as one link in a long chain stretching far into the past and far into the future.

CULTURAL INFLUENCES

But it is not only our genetic inheritance which influences us and which is a rich resource. We are also strongly influenced by the culture in which we have been brought up. Psychologists, sociologists, anthropologists and educationalists have debated long and hard over the differing influences that our genes and our environment have over us – the debate is known as that of 'nature versus nurture'. Which is the most important? Which has the most powerful impact on our character, our behaviour, the illnesses, physical and psychological, that we might develop? Although in the past some have argued for the idea that we come into life as a *tabula rasa* – a clean slate – on which society and education can write their programmes, and others have argued that we are almost totally guided by our genetic programming, the most sensible conclusions that have emerged from this debate involve different weightings being given to both influences, depending on the individual and the particular facet of his being under consideration.

How does this relate to Druidry? Druidry is concerned with the human being and his relation to the world. As such the influences which play upon him and which make him who he is are central. We know that the influence of culture upon the individual was considered important, because we know, again from archaeological evidence, that the Druid culture was highly developed. We have the evidence of the stunning achievements of the megalithic culture, with their stone constructions of engineering and mathematical skill, and we have the evidence of the Celtic culture with its beautiful artwork in jewellery, stone carving, pottery and metalwork. The classical reports speak of the cultural sophistication of the Druid system, with its divisions into Bards responsible for the arts, Ovates for prophecy, divination and healing, and Druids for law-giving, philosophy and counsel to rulers. It was not only the Spirit of the Ancestors who influenced the Druid and the common man, it was also the Spirit of the Tribe who conveyed the cultural as opposed to the familial heritage.

The Spirit of the Ancestors connects us to our individual genetic life-stream. The Spirit of the Tribe connects us to the life-stream of our culture, our tribe, our people. Today we have an interesting phenomenon taking place throughout the world. On the one hand there is a move towards a sense of One Humanity, One Tribe, One World. This has been brought about, not only by the advances in global communication, but also by the common threats of nuclear annihilation and the environmental crisis. At the same time, para- doxically, we see individual national and tribal groups trying to establish more clearly their unique identity, wanting recognition, autonomy and independence. These two trends need not be mutually exclusive. At one level we need to know that we are unique, separate beings while at another level we need to know that we are one with all beings. So it is with tribes. At one level we need to know that we belong to a particular nationality, race, cultural group or tribe and to enjoy its particularities, customs and traditions; but at another level, it is essential that we also know that we are one humanity, one people.

In modern Druidry, therefore, the Spirit of the Tribe is seen as the tribe of all humanity as well as the particular tribe we may identify with. Druidry was dogged [and still is, in some groups] with Celtic nationalism – 'we proclaim the truth against the world' was a catch-phrase, as if somehow the world was an enemy. Modern Druidry needs to recognise our need for a national, cultural and tribal identity as well as our need to know that we are one people on one earth.

It is easy for us to feel at odds with the Spirit of the Tribe. Cultural conventions, unpleasant experiences of parenting or education, restrictive or repressive cultural codes often make us rebel and live in a different manner or different country from our place of upbringing. Just as we can experience anger with our ancestors for their influence upon us, so we can also feel anger at the way our society has conditioned us. It is important that we recognise this anger and that we are able to say no to aspects of our ancestral or tribal influences which we find unhelpful or indeed harmful. But having done this, there comes a time when we can separate the wheat from the chaff and turn to the Spirit of the Tribe, as we did to the Spirit of the Ancestors, and ask to be shown its treasures, its qualities. We don't have to accept all that these worlds offer us – we are free to pick and choose. Every society has commendable aspects which we can use as nourishment and to provide us with a sense of connection to the world. If we don't approve of its mores, for example, we may still be able to feast on its art.

The allocation of the different spirits to points on the circle or to the lines of the dynamics that operate between points is not too important, and is not to be taken too literally. But in considering the Spirit of the Tribe, it should perhaps be placed at the times of Imbolc and Lughnasadh and along the dynamic that runs between them, for it is between the points of the young child and the family that environmental, tribal, influences start to work. The child is seeded at the Winter Solstice with the genetic influence which comes from its ancestors, but once it is born with this genetic endowment, environmental influences begin to play upon it, and the family is probably the single most important medium through which these cultural patterns are inculcated.

THE INFLUENCE OF PAST LIVES

Those steeped in, or familiar with, spiritual teachings and esoteric lore, will know that these two influences – recognised fully by Science – of heredity and social environment, are not the whole picture which determines who we are. There is another factor which is supremely important, and yet which is not recognised by Science, although transpersonal psychologists and certain anthropologists are beginning to research these fields. This factor is the influence that our past lives have upon us.

We know that the Druids believed in reincarnation from the classical accounts. Recognising that a powerful influence over us is the accumulated experience of previous lives, we call this stream of being or soul-essence the Spirit of the Journey. This Spirit represents the part of ourself that journeys from life to life, bringing forward each time the distilled wisdom and accumulated knowledge and experience of lifetimes. For many this Spirit lies in the Unconscious. For very good reasons most of us are unaware of it, until such time as it is awoken when we reach that point in the journey when it is safe for an awareness of its reality to emerge in everyday consciousness.

The influence of the Spirit of the Journey explains why some people are able to surmount seemingly inconquerable obstacles of genetic or environmental origin – how people born with tremendous physical handicaps or in horrendous physical conditions can emerge from them, displaying abilities and talents apparently unrelated to their genetic and cultural programming.

Part of the Druid work involves turning to the Spirit of the Journey and making connection with it, so that it can guide and counsel us. This is a subtle work which involves great care, for the Spirit of our Journey also carries our personal karma, just as the Spirit of the Ancestors carries our family karma, and the Spirit of the Tribe carries our racial karma.

Whereas the genetic and environmental vectors change with each life – for we are not always born again into the same family-stream or even the same cultural or racial stream, the past-life vector represents a continuous dynamic that carries us through each life, and for this reason it is placed in the centre of the circle.

THE INFLUENCE OF THE SPIRIT OF PLACE

It may be thought that we have covered all possible influences on the Self – our genetic and past-life inheritances together with our social, cultural, and educational conditioning. But Druidry recognises two more influences which complete the picture.

Where we are born, the locality and country in which we live are seen as powerful influences on who we are, and on how we think, feel and behave. If we live in the desert we will be different from the person who lives in the marsh-lands or the forest. Someone living in New York will have different influences playing upon them, compared with someone living in a village in Cornwall.

The Spirit of Place has always been accorded great significance in Druidry. The whole earth is considered sacred, and particular points on the earth were felt to be especially connected to certain aspects of divine power. For this reason these special spots were honoured with sacred circles of stone, with avenues or groves of trees, with monuments and with ritual. The landscape was seen as a living temple, and worship occurred, not in houses built by man, but on the sacred earth and before the open sky.

The acknowledgement of the sacredness of the landscape is a central feature of modern Druidry. We visit sacred sites, walk the ancient ley-lines, attune to the different earth-chakras and landscape temples, and open ourselves to the teaching and inspiration that comes when we commune with nature. Hill walking and camping, wilderness trekking and individual or group retreats in places of great power and beauty all provide us with a sense of deep peace and connect us to the nourishment that comes when we feel ourselves as belonging in the world, as children of the Goddess.

The Spirit of Place is truly one which can influence us profoundly. We know when we have found the right place to live or work. When we experience difficulty finding our place, attuning to this Spirit and asking for its guidance can be helpful. Deciding where to have a picnic, where to place one's bed or personal shrine in a room, or where to buy a house are all examples of situations when we can open ourselves to the Spirit of Place for guidance.

Each place has its spirit. Think of the spirit that lives at Avebury or Stonehenge, at the Great Pyramid, or in the mountains of the Himalayas. Even the corner of our garden has its spirit, and these spirits all form part of the great Spirit of Place. In astrology, our chart is not only determined by the time, but also by the place in which we are born, as determined by its longitude. Being born at noon in Perth produces a different chart to one made for a baby born at noon on the same day in Edinburgh. It is the conjunction of a particular time and place that creates the chart and which produces the planetary configurations which influence us. When we celebrate the festivals, we likewise work with a meeting of a particular time with a particular place. Our sacred circle of working, whether for a festival or for individual or group work in a grove, has its Spirit of Place, and by being aware of this, we heighten our sense of its sacredness.

Some people are drawn to working with the Spirit of Place to help purify the environment. One of the most active of these groups is Fountain International[1] – who have developed a network of groups who pray, visualise, dowse and meditate to cleanse and clear particular areas. They claim considerable success with studies showing reduced incidents of crime and accidents in areas worked upon. Individual dowsers, also, will often work on an area which is renowned for its high incidence of accidents [an accident 'black spot' on a particular road, for example]. Here they are working with the Spirit of Place, whether or not they see it in this way.

Those who visit sacred sites with intent are engaging in an age-old activity which honours the Spirit of Place. They make pilgrimages to holy sites, and this activity is known throughout the world and at all times – it is a fundamental recognition amongst all peoples of this spirit and of the necessity to honour and respect it and to draw sustenance and encouragement from it. With Islam, pilgrimages are made to Mecca. With Buddhism to such places as Mount Kailas in Tibet, and the Temple of the Sacred Tooth in Kandy, Sri Lanka. With Hinduism to the Ganges and to Benares. With Christianity pilgrimages are again a strong feature of religious life, whether for healing, as to Lourdes, or for spiritual nourishment, as to the Holy Land, Canterbury, Rome or Glastonbury. Leaving aside the major religions, we see amongst the earth religions, such as Druidry, a similar feature – wells and rivers, hills and mountains, burial sites and stone circles, lone trees and clearings in the forest, all these were and are considered sacred, and were and are the goal of conscious, dedicatory pilgrimage.[2]

An interesting exercise is to become aware of the Spirit of Place in your room or as you read this book. What does it feel like? What is its quality? Then become aware of a wider area, your town or surrounding countryside. What does it feel like now? What is its quality, its vibration? Then widen your awareness to include the whole country, asking yourself the same questions, before sensing the whole world in the same way. You can even continue it to include the whole universe, for the Spirit of Place is indeed Space Itself. Science currently estimates that the Cosmos contains three trillion galaxies, enough for each one of us to evolve to being responsible for a galaxy of our own. The Spirit of Place is truly vast for she counts all this for her realm.

In our circle we can allocate this Spirit to the line that links east and west, for our sense of space is governed to some degree by our awareness of the rising and setting sun – from 'west unto east'. The east represents those lands which are far distant and from which enlightenment comes. The west represents the 'Isles of the Blessed' – that place to which we go after death, and which is the Summerland, a haven and a place of rest and contentment.

THE INFLUENCE OF TIME

What else influences who we are? Time. The times we live in represent a fundamental influence upon who we are. In common language we talk about the Spirit of the Times, and it is clear that someone living in 1990 is under an entirely different set of influences than someone living in, say, 1590.

There is every evidence that Time was, for the Druids, an immensely important factor. Many of the stones in the stone circles are positioned so that they act as time-stones, marking the rising or setting of the mid-winter or mid-summer sun, for example. Groups of stones act as systems for other measurements, so that they can be used for predicting the times of lunar or solar eclipses, for instance.

One of the tasks of the Druid was to calculate the times for the festivals, the times for sowing and reaping, the times of eclipses and of the moon's phases. The calendar was considered extremely important, and from France we have evidence of a Druid calendrical system in the Coligny Calendar, although scholars are divided as to the degree we can consider it purely Druidic, since it is engraved in Roman letters leading some to believe it represents the product of an attempt to Romanize the native religion. Dated to the first century AD, it consists of fragments of engraved bronze which have been carefully pieced together to show a system which reckoned the beginning of each month from the full moon [a sensible idea, since a full moon is always noticeable when it appears]. Each month was divided into two periods of a fortnight, rather than into weeks. To account for the extra days which always accumulate in any calendar [we use leap years to absorb ours] they had a thirteenth month which appeared in some years and not in others. The names of the months are wonderfully evocative of a time when man lived close to nature:[3]

Seed-fall	October–November
The Darkest Depths	November–December
Cold-time	December–January
Stay-home time	January–February
Time of Ice	February–March
Time of Winds	March–April

Shoots-show	April–May
Time of Brightness	May–June
Horse-time	June–July
Claim-time	July–August
Arbitration-time	August–September
Song-time	September–October

The first eight months' names are self-evident – from the Seed-fall month of October–November when the nuts and seed-cases fall from the trees, to the Time of Brightness, when the sun reaches its maximum power at the Summer Solstice in June. Horse-time indicates the month in which one goes travelling, in the good weather, and Claim-time indicates the month in which the harvest festival of Lughnasadh falls, and at which time marriages are contracted and disputes presented before the judges. The following month, Arbitration-time in August–September, represents the time when the disputes and claims have been adjudicated and when the reckonings are given. At Song-time in September–October the bards complete their circuits and choose where they will settle for the winter season.

A study of the Coligny calendar gives us a feel for the Celtic peoples' attunement to the earth, and of the way they integrated the human affairs of travelling, adjudicating and entertaining within the yearly cycle.

Each of the eight festivals marks a conjunction of Place and Time, and it marks a special moment in the yearly cycle when the forces of nature are at their strongest in a particular direction. At the Winter Solstice these forces are accumulated deep within the soil – the seeds are fertilised by the reborn light in the darkest hour. At Imbolc the forces of growth begin to be called upward by the sun, and by the time of the Spring Equinox they are blessed with equal durations of day and night. At Beltane the call is to couple and to repeat the inexorable demand of nature that the species might flourish and continue. At the Summer Solstice the forces of the sun are at their most potent, bringing forth a burgeoning of growth at the time of maximum light and energy. At Lughnasadh, the in-gathering begins, the first of the harvest is brought in, and we accept that the energies of nature are drawing themselves back into the earth in preparation for the coming winter. At the Autumnal Equinox we sense a continuing of this process – we attune to the setting sun and the golden leaves of autumn, and feel the warm glow of recollection as we survey our lives and our year. At Samhuinn, the forces gather in completely and open out into the Other World. The cycle is complete and the Old Year ends. Time is no more, for if time was important to the Druids, then No-Time was vital too.

How do we honour the Spirit of Time in modern Druidry? Firstly, by working with the eight festivals, and by relating our own life-cycle to the natural life-cycle. In that way we slowly begin a process of reconnection to and synchronisation with nature. That harmony which our ancestors once had with the earth we can build again. Once this new sense of time and of our place within the Scheme of Time is firmly established during our period of study in the Bardic Grade, we are able to move on to the Ovate Grade, in which we approach Time in another way. One of the purposes of working with time, is to discover not only how to cooperate with it, but also how to transcend it, or travel within and through it. Why this work should be the sphere of study for the Ovate becomes clear when we realise that it is she who works with divination and prophecy – both skills which require a particular familiarity with time and an ability to render it transparent.

Time is often considered our enemy – so often we are racing against it – trying to fulfil our seemingly endless commitments within the limitations imposed by the day and its schedule. Befriending the Spirit of Time therefore reaps many benefits. The ability to create moments in our day or week when we can enter the peace of our Sacred Grove and move out of time for a moment into the vastness and the depth of No-Time and No-Thing is an ability that we come to increasingly value. On the sacred circle we relate the Spirit of Time to the vertical line travelling from the Winter Solstice to the Summer Solstice – the line that bisects the horizontal line of Space. Where the two lines meet, there is the moment of transformation of infinity and eternity, for the Spirits of Time and Place are manifestations in the physical world of the Spirits of Eternity and Infinity respectively.

If we are keen to be of value, to be of service to the world, we can discover what is needed from us, by becoming aware of the agenda that the Spirit of Time has for humanity and for the world during our lifetimes. Each period of history has had its agenda in relation to the evolution of human consciousness. We tend to think of certain individuals who stand out as great innovators and as agents for the advancement of humanity, but they have become so precisely because they have been aware of the needs of the time and have succeeded in articulating what was already fermenting in the collective psyche.

The Spirit of Time has clearly a powerful agenda for us at the moment. Events are moving at an astonishing pace as old boundaries dissolve and society moves to the very eve of the next millenium. By attuning to the Spirit, by observing what it is that is needed, and where humanity has reached in its evolution, it is possible that we can follow the advice of Bernard Shaw, a friend of the old Chief Druid, George MacGregor-Reid, when he said: 'Find out what the life force, the creative force, is working for in your time and then make for it too. In that way you become more than yourself and a part of creative evolution.'

THE FIVE FORCES

So there we have it, five Spirits which are perhaps not really spirits at all in the way that some people would understand the term, although one can often sense them as mighty Beings. Who are we to say, after all, whether or not they are spirits? Is there a being, a Spirit of Time, or are there several: Lords of Time as they are called in another tradition?

Psychologists have found, through research, that people can be roughly grouped into two categories: those who are outer-directed, who feel that their lives are controlled by outer circumstances, and those who are inner-directed, who feel that they are in control of their lives and for whom outer circumstances are subordinate. Bernard Shaw, again, provides us with a splendid quotation for inner-directedness: 'Circumstances?' He once said, 'I don't believe in circumstances. If you don't have the right circumstances in life, go out and create them!'

Of course the truth is that we are influenced by outer circumstances, but we can transcend or control them to some extent. Working in the Druid Way can help us become sensitive to the influence that each one of the five forces can have on our lives, and it can also help us to overcome any difficulties we experience as a result of their influence. The view of some historians is that the Druids and their contemporaries were engaged solely in propitiation – trying to make peace with the gods of Time and Place, Lineage and Environment through sacrifice and offerings. But the sophistication of Druid philosophy points to the fact that whilst propitiation may have been a feature of their relationship to these forces, it must also have included attunement and the acquisition of power and wisdom. It is one thing to engage in propitiation as a kind of bribe in the hope that the spirit will not harm you, and quite another to make offerings in

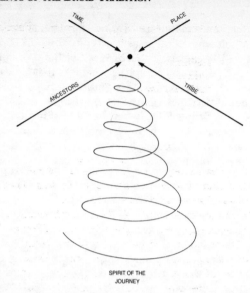

Figure 4   The Spirits of the Circle and their relationships to the Self.

the spirit of thankfulness and respect, recognising and honouring a potent force.

The trouble with modern man is that he refuses to recognise these forces, and in doing so cuts himself off from the sources of his power. The Druid turns to each of these Spirits and recognises its influence on his life. He sees their limitations and negative effects as well as their riches and benefits, and relates to them as storehouses of energy. He connects himself back into the genetic life-stream of the Ancestors, the cultural life-stream of the Tribe, the power of the earth through the Spirit of Place, the power of the times through the Spirit of Time, and the purpose of his lives through the Spirit of the Journey.

This work cannot be accomplished in a day. It is part of the long training of the Druid that is undertaken with the method that has been called 'fractional analysis' by Roberto Assagioli.[4] With fractional analysis we do not attempt to understand, face and integrate everything at once. We periodically face a particular aspect of ourselves, or in this case a particular Spirit, and gradually, fractionally, come to face, analyse and integrate more and more of its riches. In the course of this we move from being at the mercy of the family and culture we were born into, and of our geographical and temporal location, and instead we become increasingly empowered, as we are fed by

> The Richness of Place
> The Richness of Time
> The Treasures of the Tribe
> The Treasures of the Ancestors
> The Joy of the Journey

EXERCISE – 6

Having read this chapter, spend a few moments forgetting all that you have read, making yourself comfortable, and allowing yourself to come to a sense of inner centredness and calm.

Become aware of the Ancestors. See them standing before you – as if you are at the apex of a great triangle with your father and mother facing you, and their fathers and mothers standing behind them, and so on, until there are so many figures you cannot distinguish them all. Become aware of the fact that you are linked to your ancestors genetically – that a life-stream connects you to them. Notice the uncomfortable aspects of this experience. We often find the influence of our family negative, family relationships being so difficult that someone has suggested that friends are God's apology for relatives. Notice your negative reactions, if any, to your ancestors. Now see if you can open yourself to the riches that they offer you – for they carry with them a storehouse of wisdom and human experience. Say 'No' to their negative influences, but say 'Yes' to their gifts. You may find you want to enter into meditation at this stage.

When you feel ready, give thanks to your Ancestors, and see them disappearing. Feel yourself as clearly separate from them. Become fully aware of yourself here and now, before standing up and stretching.

7 · CIRCLES AND STONES TRACKWAYS AND STARS

Archaeologists for some unapparent reason had been struggling hard for many years to break the popular association of megalithic monuments with Druidism, when suddenly science restored the Druids to their old temple, Stonehenge, wiser and more venerable than before.

John Michell – *A Little History of Astro-Archaeology*

We have seen how the circle is the primal symbol of the Druid, representing the wholeness of life, its seasonal cyclicity, its completeness. We have seen how at points around the circle the Spirits that influence us are stationed, together with the four elements, the eight festivals, plants, herbs, animals and trees.

The Druids of the later period – the ones whose activities are known to us by the records of the classical authors – met, worked and taught in circular or oval-shaped clearings in the forest, which became their sacred groves. These were known by the Celtic term *Nemeton*. Tacitus in *Germania* wrote 'The grove is the centre of their whole religion. It is regarded as the cradle of the race and the dwelling-place of the supreme god to whom all things are subject and obedient.' For these later Druids, the trees marked the boundaries of the circle, and stored

*Figure 5   Stonehenge, which has been called variously The Great Circle
(Cor Gaur in ancient Cymric) The Choir of Giants (Cathoir Ghall in Gaelic)
and the Giants' Dance (Chorea Giganteum in Latin).*

the power generated within it. It was they who stood as guardians
of the sanctuary.

The earlier Druids created their sanctuaries by building circles of
stones. For the past eighty years, conventional archaeologists have
disputed this claim, rejecting the idea that circles such as Stonehenge
and Avebury ever had any connection with the Druids.

Within the received body of knowledge of Druidry it has always
been stated that the Druids built these circles, and we have seen
in Chapter One that this becomes understandable when we see the
Druid not simply as the Celtic priest of the later period, but as the
representative of a body of religious beliefs and shamanic practices
that existed from perhaps as long ago as 7000 BC up until the fifth
century AD, after which it went 'underground' before re-emerging in
the eighteenth century. A growing body of scientists and academics

now accept that the circles were built by the precursors of the Druids of classical antiquity, a group which have been termed proto-Druids but whom we term the early Druids.

The stone circles of these early Druids intrigue us – they are powerful and mysterious and call us to contemplation. To understand *why* they were built, their purpose and meaning, we need to look at *where* they were built.

In 1922 a Hereford man, Alfred Watkins, announced in a paper read to the town's Woolhope Society that he had re-discovered an ancient system of trackways, which he called leys or ley-lines. He had found that ancient sacred sites, such as standing stones, circles and tumuli, sacred trees and holy wells could be connected by straight lines which extend for many miles. These he found to coincide with prehistoric tracks, which were used in those times when people travelled across country, finding their way by walking from one landmark to the next in a straight line. He found that a notch had been cut into the ridge of a hill or a cairn had been built to act as a marker when the landscape interfered with the travellers' view of the next landmark. In time, churches were built on many of these sites, old stone crosses raised, and roads built along the trackways, so that the pattern can still be observed, plotted and even walked by those who are willing to trace the lines on an Ordnance Survey map or to follow one of the guides now available.

But the lines were not simply early man's road system. The fact that the connecting points for the tracks were sacred places shows us that man had not yet created a separation between the sacred and the profane. The utilitarian purpose of travelling was still indissolubly connected with a recognition of the sacredness of the earth and of life. The trackways probably originated in the Neolithic period, between 4000 and 2500 BC and were clearly the result of a sophisticated understanding of geomancy.

MANIFESTATIONS OF THE GREAT SPIRIT

Geomancy is known throughout the world and it can be understood as the art and science which determines the correct siting of temples, sacred circles, tombs and monuments in relation to the forces of heaven and earth. It is a knowledge of the sacredness of the earth. One of its basic tenets is that the earth carries currents of vital energy which flows in lines, just as the body carries currents of subtle energy, known to the Chinese acupuncturists as Ch'i.

The subtle energy that runs in lines across the earth can, to some extent, be measured. It is comprised of the electrical and magnetic currents which travel the earth's surface, and the radiations which emanate from underground water and mineral veins. These are the comprehensible sources of their existence, but Druidry points also to their inherently spiritual nature as manifestations of the life-force, of the Great Spirit. As such, they are conceived as pathways of Spirit, and when walked in consciousness can refresh, renew and change us. Remarkably, at the foundations of our civilisation, in the Neolithic period, we find an understanding of the inner meaning of pilgrimage.

At significant points along these arteries of the Earth-Spirit, often at junctions where several meet, we find the stone circles. Not only are they sited on leys or at junctions of leys, but they also display a number of other unusual characteristics. Dowsers have always claimed that the circles are located at spots which emit strong radiations, often finding them placed over the meeting points of underground streams.[1] Over the last ten years, a team of geologists, terrestrial magnetism and earth science specialists have been researching these sites for more specific information on their unusual characteristics.[2] Over forty stone circles have been tested with magnetometers and other instruments and they have all, without exception, been found to display anomalous natural energies when compared with their immediate surroundings. All the sites were found to be directly above or very near geological fault lines. This results in an intensification of the currents in the earth's magnetic field at these places.

Other discoveries were made. The granite in Cornwall emits such radiation that houses in certain areas must be built with radiation shields beneath the floor to protect the inhabitants' health. When the stone circles of Cornwall were tested, it was found that they acted as sanctuaries from this harmful radiation, their structure somehow creating a natural barrier or shield.

Such a 'sanctuary' effect has been noted by other researchers, but in a different way. In 1972 a zoologist who was hunting for bats at dawn one morning found his ultrasonic detector indicating a rapid and regular pulse of a powerful high-frequency signal. He allowed the detector to guide him to the source of the signal, and found himself standing at a megalithic site without a bat in sight.

The Institute of Archaeology at Oxford followed up the zoologist's observation, finding significant patterns of ultrasound at several sites with standing stones.[3] They were strongest at dawn each day, but rose to a particularly powerful emission that lasted for several hours on the mornings of the Spring and Autumn Equinoxes.

Despite this ability of certain standing stones to sound out a note, albeit inaudible to modern man, the Oxford research also discovered that stone circles, such as Stonehenge, can act as an ultrasonic barrier – creating, sometimes, complete ultrasonic silence within the circle. Again we see the circle as a place of sanctuary, as a place in which we go to find the Silence.

THE DRUID STAR WISDOM

Being located at places of unusual power on the earth's surface, at places where ley lines or underground streams meet, and where there are fault lines, and where ultrasound emissions occur at certain times and where silence pervades within the circle at other times, presents only part of the reason why stone circles are located where they are, and why they are built in their particular way.

At the beginning of this century, Sir Norman Lockyer, the astronomer and scientist and founder of *Nature* magazine, initiated the study of stone circles for their astronomical orientations. On holiday in Greece, he remembered that churches were traditionally oriented towards the point of sunrise on the feast day of their patron saint, and he decided to see whether orientation was a significant factor in the Greek temples he was visiting. His researches intrigued him and led to his determination to study the orientation of the older structures of Egypt. He travelled there in 1891 and discovered that the temple of Amen-Ra at Karnak faced the setting sun of the midsummer solstice – not in his day, but by calculation, in about 3700 BC, when the last rays of the sun would have entered the inner sanctuary at the end of the temple avenue.

The orientation of Stonehenge towards the midsummer sunrise and the midwinter sunset was already well-known, both events being visible from the centre of the circle through the narrow stone doorways or 'henges'. This led Lockyer to research Stonehenge and other megalithic sites, resulting in his publication of *Stonehenge and other British Stone Monuments Astronomically Considered* in 1906. The main conclusion that he drew from his research was that the earliest sites were laid out to mark sunrise or sunset on the quarter days of the Old Year – the days of the Celtic fire-festivals discussed in an earlier chapter. Sometimes the sites would indicate the transit of 'warning' stars that signalled the sun's appearance at these times.

This fact in itself is strong evidence for our contention that the Celtic Druids received their knowledge from the earlier Druids, the megalith builders, since the very stones themselves show that pre-Celtic man was honouring those special times of the year which later continued to be recognised by Celtic society, and later still even by Christianity. Lockyer also found that later constructions were oriented to mark the solstices – by about 1600 BC this had become the general practice amongst the circle builders.

Lockyer initiated an impulse to study the astronomical orientations of stone circles which was taken up by, amongst others, the astronomer Gerald Hawkins of Boston University. In 1965 Hawkins published *Stonehenge Decoded*, in which he detailed his discovery that by computing the extreme seasonal positions of the sun and moon in BC 1500 ten of the sighting lines and stone alignments of the monument pointed to solar azimuths and fourteen to lunar ones. He also proposed the idea that the 56 Aubrey holes at Stonehenge were used to mark the 56 years of the moon's eclipse cycle. The archaeologist Professor Atkinson attempted to debunk the idea that Stonehenge could have been constructed with these sophisticated functions in mind, but was converted to astro-archaeology, as it has come to be called, after studying the work of Professor Alexander Thom.[4] An engineer, Thom had made accurate surveys of several hundred circles and megalithic sites all over Britain. In studying these surveys, he came to the conclusion that they were all meticulously designed according to a unified standard or canon of geometry that seemed closely related to the system of mathematics that we know as Pythagorean. Since Pythagoras taught over a thousand years after the construction of these sites, it seems that the claim made by modern Druids that Pythagoras learnt his science and philosophy from the Druids, rather than vice versa, can at last be corroborated by the findings of modern science. There is a Druid adage that the truth is 'written in the stones'. It seems that the astro-archaeologists have begun to decipher this writing that has remained incomprehensible for so long.

Some commentators have assumed that the circles were used as observatories, neolithic astronomical computers, designed to predict lunar eclipses, and to indicate the correct times for festivals, and for sowing and harvesting. But to see them in this way is to understand only a small part of their purpose. Knowing that they were oriented with reference to the sun, moon and certain stars, and that they were laid out with an understanding of sacred geometry, we need then to remember that they were positioned at key points on the energy system of the earth. Their location on leys and at ley junctions combined with their orientations to the heavens rendered them able to act as 'receiving stations' for direct influences from heavenly constellations especially at certain seasons of the year. Ceremonies performed there would be immensely powerful when the Spirit of Time united with the Spirit of Place within a sanctuary created not only by the underlying geology and overarching constellations, but also by the fact that the leys, the arteries, of the Earth Spirit could both bring power to the site and also distribute the power generated there across the land.

The men and women who built and worked with these circles were clearly no barbarians. Not only did they accomplish the engineering feats necessary for their construction, but they performed these within the constraints of a sophisticated geometry and science of measurement.[5] This they combined with an understanding of energy fields to determine the circle's location, and with an understanding of astronomy to determine the siting of the individual stones.

The stones themselves were chosen with great care, often necessitating lengthy journeys from quarry to site, when different types of stone were closer to hand but clearly deemed unsuitable. Early man understood the different qualities of stone in ways that we are only just beginning to comprehend. We now know, for instance, that quartz rocks attract and store earth magnetism and electricity, and this would explain why many of the stone circles include stones with quartz.

As if the capacities of the early Druids already outlined were not enough, they showed an ability with their building of these circles to create sanctuaries of silence, wombs of timelessness surrounded by time-marking stones, and an ability to use the play of light and shadow, of sunlight and moonbeams, in a way that marks them out as our culture's first theatrical lighting designers and technicians. It must have been immensely dramatic for the Druid initiate to witness the sun rising between the trilithons at Stonehenge, or entering the inner sanctuary at New Grange at the Winter Solstice, the finger of the dawn ray gradually illuminating the rear chamber. The builders of the circles and tumuli knew that light and shadow were profoundly important, not only in the way that human consciousness can be affected by the drama of these natural phenomena, but also because they represent the two aspects of duality which are in fact one: Out of darkness is born the light and without light we could not comprehend its opposite, darkness. In the chamber of the New Grange tumulus the candidate for initiation would have waited in total obscurity within the womb of the earth at the time of the longest night of the Winter Solstice to experience a type of rebirth as the dawn rays of the rising Midwinter sun pierced the back of the chamber, heralding the rebirth of the year.

No stone circles were built after 1000 BC. We can find a number of reasons for this. There are remains of over a thousand circles to be found in Britain and Ireland. Bearing in mind that many have been destroyed by farmers clearing land, or Christians removing pagan idols, we can assume that by 1000 BC there must have been many more than the one thousand now extant. It is therefore conceivable that as saturation level was reached, the motive to build any more began to diminish. It is unlikely, however, that this was the only or even the main reason for the circles' demise. Climatic changes at this time had begun to force people off marginal land and the resulting competition for agriculturally fertile territory resulted in war and instability, forcing communities to turn away from constructing or expanding stone circles, to creating defensive structures and manufacturing weapons. As an example of this, we can see the evidence that the expansion of the Stonehenge complex ceased at about the turn of the millenium when construction work on a great two-mile earthwork-flanked avenue came to an abrupt halt.

At about this time we see the appearance of the later Druids, and it is documented that they met in sacred groves, and not in stone circles. The sacred circle was moved from the guardianship of stones to that of trees.

If we see man's spirituality as evolving, we can see a progression from meeting amongst stones to meeting amongst trees. Druids of the Revival Period met and modern Druids often meet in circles which were and are formed neither by stones nor by trees, but simply by people. Seated or standing in a circle in a room above a pub in Covent Garden in 1717, or standing on Primrose Hill in 1990, the sacred space is defined not by representatives of the mineral or plant realms but by humans. We have moved from the grossly physical world of massive stone, through the realm of the nature-spirits living in the strong and delicate trees of the grove, to the exclusively human. A cycle is finished and now the time is perhaps ripe for a return to the circles of old – only this time, as T. S. Eliot would have it, knowing the place for the first time.

EXERCISE – 7

As an exercise in relation to this chapter, you might like to visit a stone circle. When you arrive, spend a few moments calming yourself and coming to a sense of centredness, before calling to mind the ideas about circles presented in these pages. Then become aware of yourself being outside, and in full awareness step into the circle. Walk about

101

within it. How does it feel? Does it feel different inside as opposed to outside the ring of stones? What is the quality of energy here? Touch the stones, if you like, to feel their power, but remember that some stones (more usually single standing stones) were placed to draw power down into the earth to increase its fertility, and if you touch such a stone for too long you will feel drained of energy, because it was sited to absorb, not radiate, power. Most stones, however, will invigorate you. Finally, in full consciousness, step out of the circle, and notice if you feel different.

8 · DRUID TREELORE

Approaching a tree we approach a sacred being who can teach us about love and about endless giving. S/he is one of millions of beings who provide our air, our homes, our fuel, our books. Working with the spirit of the tree can bring us renewed energy, powerful inspiration, deep communion.

From the teaching material of the Ovate Grade

As we have seen from the etymology given in the Foreword, Druids were wise men of the trees. One of the world's largest tree-planting movements is called The Men of the Trees and was started by a Druid, the late Richard St Barbe-Baker.[1] Few, if any, of its members would realise that he had partly encoded the word 'Druids' in its title.

One of the reasons why the subject of Druids fascinates us, is because there is such a strong association between them and trees. If we close our eyes and imagine a Druid, we will often see him beside a tree, or within a sacred grove of trees. We sense that Druids were at one with nature in a way that we no longer are, and those of us who aspire to become Druids do so because we want to attain that at-one-ment, that union, for ourselves. In a conscious way we recognise the beauty of trees and their value to us, but just below the surface of our consciousness lies the knowledge that they also possess keys and powers that, if we were to share in them, would enrich our lives immeasurably.

TREE KNOWLEDGE – OGHAM

The Druids used a particular method for communicating and remembering their wealth of tree-knowledge. This is known as the Ogham [pronounced o'um]. It consists of twenty-five simple strokes centred on or branching off a central line. It is similar in purpose, but separate in origin from the Nordic runes. The Ogham characters were inscribed on stones or written on staves of wood. As a method of writing it is laborious, but as a language of symbolism it is powerful. It is probably pre-Celtic in origin, although most of the existing inscriptions have been dated to the fifth and sixth centuries. Whether Celtic or pre-Celtic we can sense that it carries with it some of the very earliest of Druid wisdom. Amongst our sources of information about its use, we have *The Scholar's Primer* from Scotland (transcribed from the oral tradition in the seventeenth century) and O'Flaherty's *Ogygia* from Ireland [published in 1793]. But it was the poet Robert Graves who, in modern times, brought the Ogham into public awareness once again, with his publication of *The White Goddess* in 1948.

Each stroke of the Ogham corresponds to a letter of the alphabet. This letter represents the first letter of the tree allocated to it, so that the sign ⟋ represents the letter B, and the tree Beith, the Birch. The sign ⟋ represents the letter L, and the tree Luis, the Rowan, and so on.

Although we know the letters that each stroke represents, and can translate the ancient Ogham inscriptions accordingly, we cannot be so confident when we come to associate the trees with particular months. There has been much controversy as to whether the Ogham really was used as a calendar by the Druids, linking each tree and letter of the alphabet to a moon month, as suggested by Robert Graves. Whilst it is important to be aware that there is controversy, it is also important to understand that Druidry is evolving, and that if they didn't correlate them in 500 BC they do now – if it was Robert Graves' invention, then he was acting as a Druid when he did so – he was inspired, in other words. Someone has to invent things, or 'receive' them from the invisible world, and just because he or she does so in AD 1948 rather than BC 1948 is in the final analysis unimportant to those of us who want to use Druidry as a living system, as opposed to those who want to study its origins for a purely academic purpose.

The essential point about the Druid use of Ogham is this – it provided and provides a glyph or system which is every bit as rich as the Tree of Life of the Qabalists. The Qabalists use one tree – the

Druids use a grove, a wood – filled with many trees and woodland plants. By clearly building up this wood with the inner mind and by then associating each tree or plant with a different number, god or goddess, animal, bird, colour, mineral, star, divine or human principle, the Druid is able to retain in her mind far more information than she would normally be able to, if she simply learnt lists of such facts. This use of an image as a mnemonic (memory) device has been well known as an esoteric discipline through the ages. The ancient Greeks visualised a theatre, each part of which was associated in the memoriser's mind with an item that needed remembering.[2]

But to see the Druid use of Ogham simply as a mnemonic for storing data is to fail to recognise its true purpose and value, for, having 'peopled the forest', having learnt the associations, the Druid is then able to use this network of data in just the same way that a computer can, with appropriate software, work on stored data to produce numerous combinations and recombinations. The associations start to interrelate and cross-fertilise of their own accord, even during sleep. The hard work of months and years of training starts to pay off as the Druid sleeps on (or perhaps in) her forest, and the various associations and connections between the storage points in her system start to communicate.

The method of free association used in psychoanalysis can provide a glimpse into the secret world of connections and associations that are made in the unconscious, and the particular contribution of esoteric disciplines is in providing a framework that exists partly in the conscious mind, but which also is immersed in the unconscious – allowing both aspects of the self to feed from it and to nourish it. In other words, by building a grove of trees in the imagination, or a 'Tree of Life' if one is a Qabalist, one creates a structure which operates not only in the conscious waking self, but also in the unconscious (some might say the superconscious) pulling to it, as it were, associations, ideas, images and experiences. In this way it acts as a bridge between these two parts of the self. At a deeper level the creation of such a structure allows the influx of transpersonal energies into the personal or individual psychic system in a way that is safe and structured because the channels for its reception and integration have already been built.

One of the most extraordinary things to contemplate is that as we think and make associations, our brains actually make connections and grow physically! The more we use our brain, the more dendrites (the 'arms' between brain cells) are grown, and the more synaptic connections are made (connections from the end of one dendrite to

THE ELEMENTS OF THE DRUID TRADITION

another). These neural pathways are called dendrites because they
look like the branches of a tree, and dendrite is Greek for 'tree-like'.
Photographs of sections of the cerebral cortex look like photos of a
thicket of trees in winter. So as we imagine a sacred grove of trees in
our minds and work with it over many months to create a network
of associations, we are literally building a thicker, richer complex of
connections at a physical level in our brains, as well as a structure on
a subtler level in the psyche which can connect our conscious self
with our unconscious self.

Of what trees is the Grove composed? Druids view all trees and
plants as sacred, but twenty-five trees and plants are held in particular
veneration by them. Each of these is linked with a character of the
Ogham script, with a letter of the alphabet and with a particular period
during the year.

Letter	Irish name	Tree
B	beith	birch
L	luis	rowan
F	fearn	alder
S	saille	willow
N	nuinn	ash
H	huathe	hawthorn
D	duir	oak
T	tinne	holly
C	coll	hazel
Q	quert	apple
M	muinn	vine
G	gort	ivy
NG	ngetal	broom/fern
STR	straif	blackthorn
R	ruis	elder
A	ailm	fir/pine
O	onn	gorse
U	ur	heather
E	edhadh	aspen
I	ido	yew
EA	ebhadh	aspen
OI	oir	spindle
UI	uileand	honeysuckle
IO	iphin	gooseberry
(AE)	phagos	beech

Figure 6   The Ogham Alphabet.

106

There is a certain amount of controversy over the association of some of the Ogham characters with certain of the trees, and some authors have chosen different ways of associating them with the times of the year. Those who are interested in following the intricacies of these arguments can do so by studying the relevant literature.[3] But it is important to know that no one list is absolutely and definitely the true or correct list of sacred trees, although about many there is no disagreement. Most of the controversy revolves around the allocation of the trees to the months, and since we have no physical proof of how or whether the early Druids made these connections, it seems important to allow our own inner sensibilities to guide us, and to be aware of the fact that writers disagree. The important thing is that we should establish our own personal relationship with the trees and their spirits. If we fill ourselves with other people's ideas about which trees are sacred and what properties they possess or symbolise, it tends to block our own intuitive impressions. After we have spent some time working with trees in ways that are outlined in the Ovate work, we can then turn to the different authors and see whether their insights and allocations are helpful or misleading for us.

Whilst the way that we come to a knowledge of the powers and qualities of the trees cannot be taught in a book, since it involves work outside in contact with living trees, and within one's own sacred grove with a specific sequence of exercises, we will look at some of the attributes of three trees and one sacred plant, to give an insight into their value as part of the Druid work.

BEITH – THE BIRCH TREE

The Bardic school or grade is symbolised by the Birch Tree. It is the first tree in the Ogham Cipher, and as such represents the number One. This is fitting, for it is the birch that we plant first on virgin land if we want to create a wood or forest. It is known, for this reason, as the Pioneer Tree, and it can be seen also as the tree which helps birth the forest. So it is a tree of birth – an appropriate tree to symbolise the first level of Druid working, when we are born into this new way of seeing and knowing.

The Ogham can also be used for divination,[4] and when we draw the card, or throw the disc or stave of the birch, we know that this signifies new beginnings for us, and, depending on its relative position in the spread, we know that we must either pioneer a new endeavour or that something is being given birth in our lives. Often, before we can give birth to the new, we need to cleanse ourselves of the old. Again, the birch tree is an appropriate symbol for this process of purification in preparation for new beginnings. In Scandinavia, switches of birch are used on the body to stimulate the process of purification in the sauna. In Britain the birch rod was used rather more ferociously to purify the criminal of his misdeeds, and earlier still in an attempt to expel evil spirits from 'lunatics'. In some areas, it was customary to drive out the spirits of the old year with birch switches, and throughout Europe birch twigs were used for 'beating the bounds'.

So to prepare for the new, we must free ourselves of the debris of the old, and birch can help us do this, and can point the way forward, for when we are lost in the forest, the shining whiteness of the birch trunk leads us onward – it offers guidance and orientation in the darkness of our journey. The very word 'birch' derives from a root meaning 'bright' or 'shining' in nearly all languages with Indo-European origins.

Robert Graves allocates this tree to a month stretching from 24th December to 20th January, using a calendar of thirteen lunar months, since both Caesar and Pliny reported that the Druids divided their year into lunar months. He chooses as the first month that which follows the Winter Solstice, when the year is reborn, and the days begin to lengthen. Liz and Colin Murray, authors of *The Celtic Tree Oracle*, allocate the Birch to the first month of the Celtic Year, which began at Samhuinn on 1st November.

The reasoning behind both sets of authors' allocations is clear, Graves' first month is indeed the first month of the year from the point of view of the earth's relationship with the sun in the northern hemisphere. And November was indeed the first month of the Celtic year, when the wintering-in began and the three days of Samhuinn's No-time had passed and Time was established again for the new year to come.

As with much of this work, one finds that other traditions hold many things in common. The shaman teacher of the Siberian Gold Eskimos climbs a birch tree at the high point of an initiation ceremony, circling its trunk nine times. The Buryat and the Central Asian Altai shamans carve nine notches in the trunk of a young birch, representing the steps they must take to ascend to heaven. The birch shares with the Ash the distinction of being used as a representative of the Cosmic World-Tree – the *Axis Mundi*. This tree links the Underworld with Middle Earth and Heaven Above. The shaman climbing the Birch uses it as a sky-ladder to symbolise his ability to visit other worlds.

In Britain the Birch was often used for may-poles – our version of the *Axis Mundi* around which we turn and turn. And at the same season it was the twigs of birch that were used for kindling the Beltane fire. And it was birch that was used to make babies' cradles, for if birch could drive evil from the old year, and from lunatics and criminals, it could ward off ill for the new-born too. And since birch is the tree of birthing the new, what other wood is more fitting for the newly-born?

IOHO – THE YEW TREE

As we approach the heart of the Druid Mystery, we enter the grove of the Ovates. The tree of the Ovates is the Yew.

We associate the Yew tree with death. In Britain they grow in our graveyards, and the dark green spikes of this evergreen are deadly poison. It is likely that the Latin name for this tree, *Taxus*, is the root for the word toxic. This connection with death is significant in the Druid understanding of the yew, for whereas the Bardic Grove allowed us to be reborn into a new world of understanding and expression under the sign of the Birch, as we enter the Ovate grade we come to an experience of symbolic death.

But of course death is but a gateway into greater life, a letting go in order to be reborn to a new level, and this is what is signified in the Ovate work. The yew tree, seen in this way, is the tree of both death and rebirth, and as such becomes the tree of eternity. The yew, certainly for mortal man, appears to be eternal – it can live for over two thousand years, and its guardianship of the graveyard symbolises the eternal life we return to on separation from our transient body. It signifies the mystery of transcendence over time, and whereas in the Bardic grade we worked with the central scheme of Druidry which defined the relationship of Time and Space within the mandala of the human and earthly cycles, in the Ovate Grade we travel beyond and through this frame of reference to approach the heart of timelessness.

One of the reasons for the great age of the Yew lies in the ability of its branches to grow down into the ground to form new stems which grow to become trunks of separate but linked growth. Although the central trunk becomes old and decays within, a new trunk grows inside this and eventually cannot be distinguished from the original. Because of this extraordinary method of self-renewal, the yew tree symbolises the mystery of self-transformation, renewal and rebirth – the mystery that in age we are youthful, in youth we are age-old, and that the source of our life brings perpetual renewal.

Kaledon Naddair, author of *Ogham, Koelbren and Runic*, places the Yew at the time of Midwinter. Robert Graves more precisely places the Yew on the last day of the year, at the eve of the Winter Solstice, at the time of the year's death before being reborn at the Solstice time itself. Liz and Colin Murray place it on the last day of the Old Year in the Celtic system – at the time of Samhuinn on 31st October.

In the Druid ceremony of Samhuinn a sprig of yew is distributed to each participant, indicating the yew's relationship to this time of year, our ability to commune with those who have gone before us, and our need for renewal and connection to the qualities of both release and timelessness. Drawing this card or sign on a disc or ogham stave in divination can indicate that we, or the issue in question, need to enter a period of death-and-rebirth, of letting go in order for renewal to occur.

DUIR – THE OAK TREE

With the Oak we come to the central circle of the three-fold Druid initiation. The Oak represents the Druid not only because the word Druid may well derive from words for the Oak, making the Druid the one with 'knowledge [*wid*] of the Oak [*Dru*]', but also because the Oak represents the Tree of Tradition in Druidry.

The associations to the Oak are many – he is King [or Queen] of the Forest – venerable both in age and form. The oak tree is often struck by lightning, signifying its ability to attract the energy, inspiration and illumination of the Sky Father or of the thunder-God Taran. He who has knowledge of the Oak has knowledge of the power of the elements and is able to attract the lightning-bolt of illumination from on high.

But the Oak represents also a doorway – the word door itself originates from the Gaelic and Sanskrit *duir*, meaning solidity, protection and Oak. This doorway is the entrance to the other realms. Much of Druid symbolism revolves around the concept of the entrance, gateway or door, to such an extent that the megalith builders went to enormous lengths to erect the massive stone doorways of the trilithons, as at Stonehenge, leading apparently nowhere. But the purpose of the doorway is always hidden from the uninitiate – the gateway between two trees or two stones will for one person be nothing but an empty space, but for the Druid will be the means whereby she can enter another state of consciousness, another realm of being. The secret 'oaken door' figures in the poems of Taliesin, and it is through this door that we encounter faerie beings and inner worlds of great beauty and power.

Figure 7   A Moccas Park Oak – drawn by J. Strutt in 1830. Immortalised by the naturalist Francis Kilvert in the nineteenth century, Moccas Park in the Welsh borders, is one of the finest examples of wood parkland in Britain. Kilvert's oaks – the 'grey old men of Moccas ... (which) look as if they had been at the beginning and making of the world' are well over five hundred years old and are amongst the best specimens of this tree revered by the Druids.

  The Oak symbolises not only the ability to receive sudden illumination from above, or entrance to another world through its doorway, it also symbolises strength, solidity, continuity of tradition, and endurance. Although not as long-living as the Yew, the Oak often lives for over five hundred years, and frequently stood at the hub of a village as a symbol of its age and continuity. The Oak was thus a tree that acted as a gathering-place for the populace – a remnant of the tradition that Druids taught under the Oak tree. And it was Edward the Confessor who seemed to respond to this awareness of the Oak as a sacred tree of meeting. by renewing the City of London's charter and swearing his oath upon the gospels at Gospel Oak in Highgate.
  Oak forests covered Britain and much of Europe, groves of oak trees would therefore have been numerous and the Oak would have represented one of the most prominent and numerous of early man's trees. The Oak was personified as the Oak King, the god of the waxing

year from the time of the Winter Solstice to the Summer Solstice. At midsummer he would do battle with the Holly King, who would then rule the waning year until the Winter Solstice, at which time the supremacy would revert once more to the Oak King. Midsummer fires were of oak, and midsummer is the time of the oak's flowering, and since it is also the central tree of Druid Tradition, Robert Graves places it at the centre of the year, in the month running from 10th June to 7th July – a time ruled by Jupiter, the oak-god. Like Janus, the Oak looks both ways at the centre-point of the year:back to the past of the year and forward to its future.

In Liz and Colin Murray's scheme, the Oak is also the central month of the year, standing in the seventh of thirteen months. By beginning their year in November, however, the Oak month falls in May, which seems to have less relevance than the midsummer month chosen by Graves. One connection with May, however, is that the Oak was also the tree of the Celtic god Dagda, and it was the Dagda who supervised the boiling of a great cauldron of plenty, prototype of the grail, stirring it with a wooden spoon large enough to hold a man and woman coupled together. Here the Dagda, the spoon and the cauldron are seen as symbols of the fecundity of life and it is at Beltane in May that the fundamental sexuality of nature becomes apparent in the flowering of the earth and in the coupling of both man and beast.

The connection between this coupling and the mysteries of time and generation will become clearer when we examine a plant that has sometimes been connected with the Ogham Cipher, but which has always been connected with Druidry – the mistletoe.

MISTLETOE

The association of Druids with mistletoe is strong in the popular mind, and not without good reason. Pliny, in his *Natural History*, spoke of the Druid custom of gathering mistletoe:

> The druids, for so call they their Magi, have nothing more sacred than the mistletoe, and the tree on which it grows, provided it be the oak. They select a particular grove of oaks and perform no sacred rites without oak leaves, so that from this custom they may seem to have been called Druids (Oakites), according to the Greek interpretation of that word. They reckon whatever grows on these trees is sent down from Heaven and a proof that the tree itself is chosen by Deity. But the mistletoe is very rarely found and when found is sought after with the greatest religious ardour, and principally in the sixth moon, which is the beginning of their months and years, and when the tree is thirty

years old it is then not half-grown only but has attained its full vigour. They call it All-Heal (Ull-ice) by a word in their own language and having proper sacrifices and feasts under the trees with great solemnity bring up two white bulls, whose horns are then first bound. The priest, clothed in a white surplice, ascends the tree and cuts it off with a golden knife, and it is received in a white sheet. Then they sacrifice the victims and pray that God would render his own gifts prosperous to those on whom He has bestowed it. They reckon the mistletoe administered as a potion can impart fecundity to any barren animal and that it is a remedy against all kinds of poison.

To understand the reason for the Druid's reverence for mistletoe we need to realise that they considered the union of the mistle with the oak deeply symbolic, as they likewise considered the cutting of it with a golden sickle, and its falling to the ground.

The mistletoe is symbolically related to the male sperm due to the colour and consistency of the mistleberry juice. Being airborne, the mistletoe has not touched the ground, it symbolises, therefore, seed-in-potency, in potential, awaiting the moment of conception. When the mistletoe was cut at the time of the Winter Solstice and brought down from the tree, the Druid was enacting the process of incarnation, of fertilisation, of conception. The airborne seed symbolises the divine spark of individuality, of God. It has not yet incarnated on earth, it has had no contact with earth, it is still on the World-Tree, at the top, close to Heaven. The Druid cuts it down with the golden sickle – with sun and moon, male and female power, united. Conjunction, union, having occurred, the spark is drawn down into the body, into life on earth, as it is brought down from the tree. And of course it is no coincidence that this occurred at the

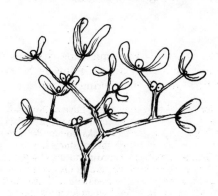

Figure 8   Mistletoe

time of the Solstice, when the sun is reincarnated, or in the Christian tradition when the son is incarnated.

The mistletoe symbolises the moment of incarnation, the moment of entry-into-time. The oak symbolises the eternity of Tradition. Oak and mistle united point to the mystery of the existence of both Time and No-Time, Form and No-Form.

In the Druid ceremony of Alban Arthuan, at the Winter Solstice, the mistletoe on the altar is, at the end, distributed to all present as a token and talisman for the times to come. We see an interesting survival of this custom in certain Christian churches: at York Cathedral a branch of mistle remained on the high altar for the twelve days of Christmas. In Wolverhampton and Staffordshire a similar tradition is recorded, the mistle being distributed afterwards to the congregation.

The connection between the mistle and fertilisation, or fertility, is with us still when we hang up the mistle-bunches at Christmas that allow us to kiss beneath them.

EXERCISE – 8

As an exercise in relation to this chapter, you might like to allow yourself to develop a relationship with a particular tree. Feel if you can notice how far its 'aura' or energy field extends. Experiment by walking backwards and forwards from it, until you can feel the extent of its subtle influence. Ask permission to attune with the tree, and spend time meditating beneath it, opening yourself to its inspiration.

AFTERWORD

Turning around and around in a circle,
Spiralling towards the centre,
We know that we have come to the centre of who we are.
We crouch on the earth, we touch her with our hands.
We know that we have come to be with her.
Finding ourselves we have found our connection with Nature.
We sing, we speak poetry, we chant, we make music —
Finding our hearts we have found the heart of the mystery.
Finding the depths we have found the Way to be simple.

Druidry is not complicated path. It may not even be a path. Appreciating it involves reorienting oneself so that one can approach the mysterious, the feminine, the Arts, both aesthetic and esoteric, in a way that allows us to let go of our assumptions and presumptions about life and instead carries us, as in a Druid ceremony, around the circle of our life towards the still point at the centre of which is both our True Self and the Divine Source.

The Call to this way is being heard again throughout the world, because it represents, not an eccentric, irrelevant and atavistic belief-system, but an approach to life that can unite the spiritual and the artistic, the environmental and the humanitarian concerns we share, the thirst for connection with Mother Earth and with Father Sun — the need for a powerful, pure spirituality and the need for a down-to-earth, sensual, fully human connection with our bodies and the body of our home, the Earth.

One of the most moving moments that can occur on our spiritual and psychological journey is the discovery that in our hearts lies a wounded child. However careful our upbringing might have been, it seems inevitable that we first experience this inner child as hurt and rejected. Once, however, we open ourselves to him or her, no longer pretending or living as if s/he didn't exist, we find that a further level peels away, to reveal that the child within is in fact a Divine child, a radiant seed-being of God/dess. Within a Christian framework we can say that we experience the reality and the presence of the Christ-child within our hearts. The Druid tradition speaks of the same mystery, but calls the child the Mabon.

In a peculiar reflection of the story of the Prodigal Son, it is we as adults who turn to the Child to recognise him as the manifestation of Divinity within us. And it is we as adults who come to understand that the negativity and the destruction that we experienced and expressed came from the desperation of the wounded child who needed to be heard. In our struggle to 'grow up' we ignored the voice that became buried deeper and deeper in our hearts.

A similar process of burial has occurred on a collective level. Beneath the cathedrals of St Paul's in London and Notre-Dame in Paris lie stone circles, forgotten by a culture who has denied its roots. The consequences of this denial have made modern man act in a way that Thomas Berry suggests is like that of the autistic child – the child who cannot face the world, and who seems not to see or hear even though we know he can. He is emotionally isolated from his fellow creatures but is fascinated by mechanical devices. We, as a culture, are obsessed with mechanics, we no longer hear the voice of the river or the sea, we can no longer let the 'outer world flow into our beings'. Berry continues by suggesting:

> Perhaps nothing is more difficult for those of us who live within the Western biblical-classical tradition. Throughout the entire course of this tradition, the autism has deepened with our mechanism, our political nationalism, and our economic industrialism. Presently a new interpretation of the Western historical process seems to be indicated. Neither the liberal progressive nor the conservative traditionalist seems to fit the situation. The only suitable interpretation of Western history seems to be the ironic interpretation. This irony is best expressed, perhaps, by the observation that our supposed progress toward an ever-improving human situation is bringing us to wasteworld instead of wonderworld.'[1]

Unconsciously or consciously we have despised our origins because we believed ourselves to have been savage brutish beings. In the same way we unconsciously despise the child who lives in our hearts because he is a whining, weak and ignorant creature. But the stone which has been rejected shall be the cornerstone of the temple. When we turn to the child and see him for who he really is he becomes our saviour, and when we turn to our past and see it for all that it really represents, it in turn has the potential to become the saviour of humanity.

At the beginning of this book I suggested that the study of Druidry can be considered as cultural therapy. We have seen that we can approach it with either of two opposing premises. Our ancestors are seen either as barbarian, primitive and ignorant, living in a world 'nasty, brutish and short' or as wise, noble philosophers and mystics, versed in mathematics, engineering, philosophical and astronomical surveying skills.

In the first view of Druidry, we espouse the theory of Original Stupidity seeing man struggling from the darkness of prehistoric ignorance to the light of present-day scientific knowledge. The second view recognises that our foundations grew out of an age of light rather than darkness.

The way we view our origins determines the way we relate to the world. Pelagius, born *circa* AD 360 was a British theologian who challenged the concept of Original Sin. Some say he was a Druid. We cannot be sure whether he was or not, but he was certainly deeply influenced by their heritage.[2] He taught the doctrine of Original Blessing, insisting that a baby is born blessed and innocent rather than sinful. He was persecuted by the Church and chased out of Europe, dying *circa* AD 430 either in Africa or the Middle East, though some say he might have found refuge in his last years in a monastery in Wales.

In our own day the Vatican has attempted to silence the brilliant theologian Matthew Fox who also teaches the doctrine of Original Blessing.[3]

The time has come for the return of the repressed. The time has come for us to fully acknowledge that our Origins, our source and our basis, are Divine.

Our roots are holy.

NOTES

FOREWORD

1. Speech to the North American Conference on Religion and Ecology in Washington, 18 May 1990.
2. Until recently, the only way to learn about Druidry was to personally visit a Druid or belong to a working group. So that more people could benefit from Druidry, a postal course was developed, and details are given in the Resources section. For information on the origin of the course see the Foreword in *The Book of Druidry*, 1990, and the essay 'Why Druids Now?' in *Voices from the Circle – The Heritage of Western Paganism*, 1990.

INTRODUCTION

1. In 1989 an annual conference was established to provide a forum for Christians and Druids to meet and discuss topics of mutual interest and areas of disagreement. Chiefs and members of many of the Druid Orders meet over three days with writers such as John Michell and Shirley Toulson and both lay and ordained Christians.
2. William Irwin Thompson, *The Time Falling Bodies Take To Light*, 1981.

1. WHO WERE THE DRUIDS?

1. Caitlín Matthews, *The Elements of the Celtic Tradition*, 1989.
2. Kenneth Jackson, *The Oldest Irish Tradition: A Window on the Iron Age*, 1964.
3. Myles Dillon, *Early Irish Literature*, 1948.

4. The *Mabinogion* represents a treasure house for those wishing to understand the British Mysteries. A modern translation is available by J. Gantz [Penguin 1976]. To fully appreciate its value, a reading of the stories should be combined with a study of Caitlín Matthews' two workbooks: *Mabon and the Mysteries of Britain*, 1987, and *Arthur and the Sovereignty of Britain*, 1989.

5. The Book of Taliesin can be found in the Lady Charlotte Guest translation of the *Mabinogion*, published by Llanerch, 1989. Our understanding of this is deepened if we also study John Matthews' *Taliesin – Shamanism and the Bardic Mysteries in Britain and Ireland*, 1991 and *The Song of Taliesin*, 1991.

6. *Trioedd Ynys Prydein*, gathered and translated by Rachel Bromwich, 1961.

7. Jean-Pierre Mohen, *The World of Megaliths*, 1989.

8. See Ch. IX, Colin Renfrew, *Archaeology and Language*, 1989.

9. Ibid.

10. Ibid.

11. See Alwyn and Brinley Rees, *Celtic Heritage*, 1989; Anne Ross, *Pagan Celtic Britain*, 1967; and W. D. O'Flaherty, *Women, Androgynes and Other Mythical Beasts*, 1980.

2. The Recent Past

1. Stuart Piggott, *The Druids*, 1985.

2. See Ross Nichols, *The Book of Druidry*, 1990.

3. Jules Michelet, *La Sorcière*, 1862.

4. See references to festivals in the Select Bibliography.

5. See Anne Ross, *Pagan Celtic Britain*, 1967. Such a community is fictionally depicted in the Canadian author Charles deLint's book *Green Mantle*, 1988. Examples of the reality of traditional communities can be found in Rhiannon Ryall, *West Country Wicca*, 1989, and in the article 'Breaking the Circle' by John Matthews in *Voices from the Circle – The Heritage of Western Paganism*, 1990.

6. Charles MacLean, *Island on the Edge of the World*, 1983.

7. Rupert Sheldrake, *A New Science of Life*, 1985.

8. Thomas Hobbes, *Leviathan*, 1651.

9. Peter Martyr, 1511.

10. Stuart Piggott, *The Druids*, 1985.

11. Ross Nichols, *The Book of Druidry*, 1990.

12. *An Tigh Geatha Gairdeachas* [Gaelic] means 'The Grove of the Gatehouse'.

3. Who Are Druids Now?

1. The Fellowship of Isis. Details of which are obtainable from the FOI, Clonegal Castle, Enniscorthy, Eire.

2. *Prophet, Priest and King — the Poetry of Ross Nichols*, edited by Jay Ramsay, 1991.
3. Starhawk, *Dreaming the Dark — Sex, Magic and Politics*, and *The Spiral Dance*, 1979.
4. The Ancient Order of Druids has a few female-only lodges, but the sexes are able to mix at certain social events. Moves may be afoot to desegregate the lodges.

4. BARDS, OVATES AND DRUIDS

1. *Auraicept na N'Eces* [The Scholar's Primer] ed. G. Calder, Edinburgh, 1917.
2. John Lilly, *The Centre of the Cyclone*, 1973.
3. From Jay Ramsay, *For Now*, 1991.
4. Michael Harner, *The Way of the Shaman*, 1980.
5. See Maria-Begel Wosein, *Sacred Dance*, 1972.
6. See *The Circle of Sacred Dance — Peter Deunov's Paneurythmy*, ed. David Lorimer, 1991.
7. See Schwarz, Schweppe and Pfau, *Wyda, Die Kraft der Druiden*, 1989.
8. Transformation, ed. Jay Ramsay, 1987.
9. See Margot Grey, *Return from Death*, 1985, and David Lorimer, *Survival? Body, Mind and Death in the Light of Psychic Experience*, 1984.
10. See R. J. Stewart, *The Prophetic Vision of Merlin*, 1986.
11. Stuart Piggott, *The Druids*, 1985.
12. Caitlín Matthews, *The Elements of the Celtic Tradition*, 1989.
13. Julius Caesar, *De Bello Gallico* VI, 13.
14. E. Hull, *The Folklore of the British Isles*, 1928, pp. 272–3.
15. The complete text of this ritual is given in Ross Nichols, *The Book of Druidry*, 1990.
16. Julius Caesar, *De Bello Gallico* VI, 14.

6. SPIRITS OF THE CIRCLE

1. *Fountain International* — a charity concerned with planetary and community healing applied directly through the Earth's energy fields, its focal centres and connecting alignments: PO Box 915, Seaford, E. Sussex, BN25 1TW.
2. A modern group in Britain which is concerned with the value and practice of pilgrimage in a way that is not tied to any one religion or belief-system and which organises pilgrimages and related events in connection with sacred sites, earth chakras, holy places and landscape temples is: *The Gatekeeper Trust*, Roses Farmhouse, Epwell Road, Tysoe, Warwickshire, CV35 0TN.
3. Translated by Caitlín Matthews in *The Elements of the Celtic Tradition*, 1989.
4. Roberto Assagioli introduced Psychosynthesis as a way of understanding

the human being and as a method of psychotherapy. See Will Parfitt, *The Elements of Psychosynthesis*, 1991.

7. CIRCLES AND STONES – TRACKWAYS AND STARS

1. See Tom Graves, *Needles of Stone Revisited*, 1986.
2. The results of this research are summarised in Paul Devereux, *Places of Power* 1990, and *Earthlights Revelation*, 1989
3. See D. Robins, *The Dragon Project and the Talking Stones*, New Scientist 21 October, 1982.
4. A. Thom, *Megalithic Sites in Britain*, 1967.
5. See Keith Critchlow, *Time Stands Still*, 1979.

8. DRUID TREELORE

1. See Richard St. Barbe-Baker, *My Life, My Trees*, 1985.
2. See Frances Yates, *Theatre of The World*, 1969.
3. See Robert Graves, *The White Goddess*, 1948, Liz and Colin Murray, *Celtic Tree Oracle*, 1989, and Kaledon Naddair, *Ogham, Koelbren and Runic* Vols. I and II, 1986. Privately published by Keltia Publications, 4a Minto Street, Edinburgh, EH7 4AN.
4. See Resources section for contemporary presentations of this method.

AFTERWORD

1. Thomas Berry, *The Dream of the Earth*, 1990.
2. See M. Forthomme Nicholson 'Celtic Theology: Pelagius' in *An Introduction to Celtic Christianity*, ed. James P. Mackey, 1989.
3. See Matthew Fox, *Original Blessing*, 1989.

RESOURCES

'But we shall never understand Druidism . . . unless we grasp the fact that it was recognised that all knowledge must be sought in two directions: one, by searching the outer world – *Science*; and two, by searching the depths of the human soul and the secrets of the human body – *Art*.'

Eleanor Merry – *The Flaming Door*

If you are interested in studying the Druid Way, the most effective approach is to take a workshop or training course, combined with reading from the Select Bibliography. In this way you can gain first-hand experience of Druidry, as well as intellectual knowledge.

COURSES AND GROUPS:

The Order of Bards, Ovates and Druids runs an experientially-based postal course and workshops in Druidry, together with a Sacred Tree planting programme and the Campaign for Individual Ecological Responsibility. Details from: OBOD, 260 Kew Road, Richmond, Surrey, TW9 3EG.

The College of Druidism, 4a Minto Street, Edinburgh, EH7 4AN, offers a correspondence course on Druidry, together with various publications.

Chrysalis – Awakening the Poet Within, 4 Farlow Road, London SW15 1DT. An experientially-based postal course and workshop programme for those who wish to develop their Bardic skills in a modern context.

CARD SETS

Using the following sets, which draw on the Druidic and Celtic wisdom traditions, can provide experiences of these traditions in deeper ways than book study:

The Celtic Tree Oracle – works with the sacred trees of the Celts and Druids and the Ogham, mentioned in Chapter Eight. Liz and Colin Murray, Rider, 1989.

The Arthurian Hallows – works with the Arthurian and Grail mysteries to create a path of self-discovery. John and Caitlin Matthews, Aquarian, 1990.

Koelbren and Ogham Divination Sets – are available from Kaledon Naddair, Keltia Publications, 4a Minto Street, Edinburgh, Scotland EH7 4AN.

Ogham Divination Sets – made of wooden staves are available from Herman Turner, Killoughter Road, Galway, Eire.

The Merlin Tarot – a book and card set by R. J. Stewart. Aquarian, 1988.

TEXTS

Most of the key tests produced during the revival period of Druidry, in the eighteenth and nineteenth centuries, are now out of print. But copies of many of these can be obtained from: The Banton Press, 75 Nelson Street, Largs, Ayrshire, Scotland KA30 9AB.

SELECT BIBLIOGRAPHY

THE HISTORY OF DRUIDRY

Chadwick, Nora K. *The Druids*, University of Wales Press, 1966
Elder, I. H. *Celt, Druid and Culdee*, Covenant, 1986.
Kendrick, T.D. *The Druids*, Cass, 1927
Nichols, Ross, *The Book of Druidry – History, Sites, Wisdom*, Aquarian Press, 1990
Owen, A.L. *The Famous Druids*, Greenwood Press, 1962
Piggott, Stuart, *The Druids*, Thames & Hudson, 1985
Rutherford, Ward *The Druids*, Aquarian Press, 1983
Spence, Lewis *The History and Origins of Druidism*, Aquarian, 1973

THE FESTIVALS

Bloom, William *Sacred Times – A New Approach to Festivals*, Findhorn Press, 1990
Bord, Janet and Colin *Earth Rites*, Paladin, 1982
Cooper, Jean *The Aquarian Dictionary of Festivals*, Aquarian Press, 1989
Farrar, Janet and Stewart *Eight Sabbats for Witches*, Hale, 1981
Green, Marian *A Harvest of Festivals*, Longman, 1980
Knightly, Charles *The Customs and Ceremonies of Britain*, Thames & Hudson, 1986
MacNeill, Maire *The Festival of Lughnasa*, Oxford University Press, 1962
Toulson, Shirley *The Winter Solstice*, Jill Norman & Hobhouse, 1981

CIRCLES, CITIES, SITES AND STONES

Atkinson, R.J.C. *Stonehenge*, Hamish Hamilton, 1956

Bord, Janet and Colin, *Mysterious Britain*, Paladin, 1974

—*The Secret Country*, Paladin, 1978

Brennan, Martin, *The Stars and The Stones*, Thames & Hudson, 1982

Chippindale Devereux, Fowler, Jones and Sebastian, (eds.) *Who Owns Stonehenge?* Batsford, 1990

Cooke, Grace and Ivan *The Light in Britain*, White Eagle Publishing Trust, 1971

Critchlow, Keith *Time Stands Still*, Gordon Fraser, 1979

Devereux, Paul *Earthlights Revelation*, Blandford, 1989

—*Places of Power*, Blandford, 1990

—and Ian Thomson *The Ley Hunter's Companion*, Thames & Hudson, 1979

Graves, Tom *Needles of Stone Revisited*, Gothic Image, 1986

Hawkins, G.S. *Stonehenge Decoded*, Souvenir Press, 1966

Howard, Michael *Earth Mysteries*, Hale, 1990

Joussaume, Roger *Dolmens for the Dead – Megalith building throughout the world*, Batsford, 1988

Lehrman, Frederic, (ed.) *The Sacred Landscape*, Celestial Arts Publishing, USA, 1988

Macleod, Fiona *Iona*, Floris Books, 1982

Matthews, John and Chesca Potter, (eds.) *The Aquarian Guide to Legendary London*, Aquarian Press, 1990

Michell, John, *New Light on the Ancient Mystery of Glastonbury*, Gothic Image, 1990

—*The New View Over Atlantis*, Thames & Hudson, 1983

—*The Earth Spirit, its Ways, Shrines and Mysteries*, Thames & Hudson, 1975

—*A Little History of Astro-Archaeology*, Thames & Hudson, 1989

Miller and Broadhurst *The Sun and the Serpent*, Pendragon, 1990

Mohen, Jean-Pierre *The World of Megaliths*, Cassell, 1989

Newman, Paul *Gods and Graven Images – the Chalk Hill-figures of Britain*, Hale, 1987

Pennick, Nigel, and Devereux, Paul *Lines on the Landscape*, Hale, 1990

Renfrew, Colin, (ed.) *The Megalithic Monuments of Western Europe*, Thames & Hudson, 1983

Screeton, Paul *Quicksilver Heritage*, Thorsons, 1974

Stewart, R.J. and Matthews, John *Legendary Britain – An Illustrated Journey*, Blandford Press, 1989

Street, C.E. *Earthstars – The geometric groundplan underlying London's ancient sacred sites and its significance for the New Age*, Hermitage Publishing, PO Box 1383, London, N14 6LF. 1990.

Thom, A. *Megalithic Sites in Britain*, Oxford University Press, 1967

Ucko, P.J., Hunter, M., Clark, A.J., and David, A. *Avebury Reconsidered. From the 1660s to the 1990s.*, Unwin Hyman, 1990

Watkins, Alfred *The Old Straight Track*, Abacus, 1974
—*The Ley Hunter's Manual*, Aquarian, 1989

RELATED STUDIES

Adler, Margot *Drawing Down the Moon*, Beacon Press, 1979
Bancroft, Ann *Origins of the Sacred*, Arkana, 1987
Berry, Thomas *The Dream of the Earth*, Sierra Club Books, San Francisco, 1990
Bromwich, Rachel [trans.] *Trioedd Ynys Prydein*, University of Wales Press, 1961
Calder, George, (ed.) *Auraicept na N'Eces [The Scholar's Primer]*, Edinburgh, 1917
Carmichael, A. (ed.) *Carmina Gadelica*, Scottish Academic Press, 1972
deLint, Charles *Green Mantle*, Ace Books, New York, 1988
Dillon, Myles *Early Irish Literature*, University of Chicago Press, 1948
Fox, Matthew *Original Blessing*, Bear & Co., 1989
Graves, Robert *The White Goddess*, Faber & Faber, 1961
Green, Marian *The Path through the Labyrinth*, Element Books, 1988
Green, Marian *The Elements of Natural Magic*, Element Books, 1989
Grey, Margot *Return from Death*, Arkana, 1985
Hartley, Christine *The Western Mystery Tradition*, Aquarian Press, 1968
Harner, Michael *The Way of the Shaman*, Harper & Row, 1980
Howe, Graham *The Mind of the Druid*, Skoob, 1990
Hull, E. *The Folklore of the British Isles*, 1928
Jackson, Kenneth *The Oldest Irish Tradition: a Window on the Iron Age*, Cambridge, 1964
Jones, Prudence and Matthews, Caitlín [eds] *Voices from the Circle – The Heritage of Western Paganism*, Aquarian, 1990
Lilly, John *The Centre of the Cyclone*, Paladin, 1973
Lindfield, Michael *The Dance of Change, an Eco-Spiritual Approach to Transformation*, Arkana, 1986
Lorimer, David *Survival? Body, Mind and Death in the Light of Psychic Experience*, Routledge & Kegan Paul, 1984
—[ed.] *The Circle of Sacred Dance – Peter Deunov's Paneurythmy*, Element Books, 1991
Mackey, James, (ed.) *An Introduction to Celtic Christianity*, Clark, Edinburgh, 1989
MacLean, Charles *Island on the Edge of the World – The story of St. Kilda*, Canongate, 1983
Markale, Jean *Women of the Celts*, Inner Traditions, 1986
Matthews, Caitlín *The Elements of the Celtic Tradition*, Element Books, 1989
—*Mabon and The Mysteries of Britain*, Arkana, 1987
—*Arthur and the Sovereignty of Britain – King and Goddess in the Mabinogion*, Arkana, 1989
Matthews, John *Taliesin – Shamanism and the Bardic Mysteries in Britain and Ireland*, Aquarian, 1991

—*The Song of Taliesin*, Mandala, 1991

—*The Celtic Shaman*, Element Books, 1991

Matthews, John and Caitlín *The Western Way*, Arkana, 1985

Merry, Eleanor C. *The Flaming Door – The Mission of the Celtic Folk-Soul*, Floris Books, 1983

Michelet, Jules *La Sorcière*, 1862

Murray, Liz and Colin *The Celtic Tree Oracle*, Rider, 1989

Naddair, Kaledon *Keltic Folk & Faerie Tales*, Century, 1987

—*Ogham, Koelbren and Runic* [2 vols.] Keltia, 1986

O'Flaherty, W.D. *Women, Androgynes and Other Mythical Beasts*, University of Chicago Press, 1980

Parfitt, Will *The Elements of Psychosynthesis*, Element Books 1990

Piggott, Stuart *William Stukeley*, Thames & Hudson, 1985

—*Ancient Britons and the Antiquarian Imagination*, Thames & Hudson, 1989

Poynder, Michael *Pi in the Sky*, Grosvenor Publishing, 1991

Ramsay, Jay, (ed.) *Prophet, Priest and King – A Selection of Ross Nichols' Poetry*, Element Books, 1991

Ramsay, Jay and Godbert, Geoffrey *For Now*, Diamond Press, 1991

Rees, Alwyn and Brinley Rees, *Celtic Heritage*, Thames & Hudson, 1989

Renfrew, Colin *Archaeology and Language – The Puzzle of Indo-European Origins*, Penguin, 1989

Ross, Anne *Pagan Celtic Britain*, Routledge & Kegan Paul, 1967

—*The Life and Death of a Druid Prince*, Rider, 1989

Ryall, Rhiannon *West Country Wicca*, Phoenix Publishing, 1989

Schwarz, Schweppe and Pfau *Wyda Die Kraft der Druiden*, Bauer, Freiburg 1989

Sheldrake, Rupert *A New Science of Life*, Anthony Blond, 1985

Spence, Lewis *The Mysteries of Britain*, Aquarian, 1970

Starhawk *Dreaming the Dark – Sex, Magic and Politics*,

—*The Spiral Dance*, Harper & Row, 1979

Stewart, R.J. *The Prophetic Vision of Merlin*, Arkana, 1986

—*The Underworld Initiation*, Aquarian, 1985

Thompson, William Irwin *The Time Falling Bodies Take to Light – Mythology, Sexuality and the Origins of Culture*, Rider Hutchinson, 1981

Toulson, Shirley *The Celtic Alternative – A reminder of the Christianity we lost*, Century, 1987

Watson, Lyall *Neophilia – The Tradition of the New*, Sceptre, 1989

Wosein, Maria-Begel *Sacred Dance*, Thames & Hudson, 1972

Yates, Frances *Theatre of the World*, Routledge & Kegan Paul, 1969

INDEX

128